RAINY DAY FUN

CRAFTS AND ACTIVITIES

Publications International, Ltd.

Contributing writers: Karen E. Bledsoe, Jamie Gabriel, Kersten Hamilton, Rita Hoppert, Ed.D., Lisa Lerner, Candyce Norvell, Stan and Shea Zukowski

Contributing illustrators: Terri and Joe Chicko, Jim Connolly, Susan Detrich, John Jones

Additional images from Shutterstock.com

ISBN: 978-1-64558-609-8

Manufactured in China.

8 7 6 5 4 3 2 1

SAFETY WARNING

All of the experiments and activities in this book MUST be performed with adult supervision. All projects contain a degree of risk, so carefully read all instructions before you begin and make sure that you have safety materials such as goggles, gloves, etc. Also make sure that you have safety equipment, such as a fire extinguisher and first aid kit, on hand. You are assuming the risk of any injury by conducting these activities and experiments. Publications International, Ltd. will not be liable for any injury or property damage.

Let's get social!
@Publications_International
 @PublicationsInternational
www.pilbooks.com

CONTENTS

WHEN IT RAINS, IT POURS

It's raining, it's snowing, or it's just plain cold and gloomy outside. Now what can you do to keep the kids entertained and happy? Pull out *Rainy Day Fun*, that's what! This fun-filled, imaginative book is packed with great ideas for crafts and activities that are educational as well as entertaining. Many foster group participation in a way that contributes to family unity or friendship fun. Still others stimulate the imagination, encouraging creative thinking.

In keeping with the idea that these are activities and projects children will choose to do at the last minute, when rainy weather limits or cancels their alternate plans, we have tried to select only projects that call for materials commonly found around the house or those that are easily accessible. We've also tried to include projects and activities that can be completed in a short amount of time.

Rainy Day Fun is divided into four chapters: Art Projects, Craft Activities, Science and Nature Projects, and Holiday Crafts.

In Chapter 1 (Art Projects), children are introduced to many art techniques. Some are basic (painting, sponging); others are more "exotic" (papier mâché, paper folding, mixing medias). Easy-to-follow instructions quickly demystify even the most ambitious-sounding projects.

Chapter 2 (Craft Activities) features projects that employ art skills introduced in Chapter 1. Children will learn how to use various tools while experimenting with different ideas. Each child creates their own additions that make each project unique.

Chapter 3 (Science and Nature Projects) offers the excitement of discovery, the joy of beauty, and the thrill of learning. What child doesn't love to explore the mysteries of the world around them?

In Chapter 4 (Holiday Crafts), children will use new skills and techniques to create impressive projects throughout the whole year.

Each activity includes a list of materials needed to complete the project as well as easy-to-follow instructions. Take the time to go over the instructions carefully, and make sure you've got all the materials on hand before you get started. The projects range in difficulty.

While many projects fit into one category, some processes cut across chapters. Cut-and-paste and coloring skills are part of almost all the chapters. Another crossover theme is an adult's supervision of children's play. Kids will need help with some projects, such as baking in an oven or cutting with a craft knife. Other projects require only a watchful eye. You know your child. A five-year-old needs more supervision than a ten-year-old, but even within one age, two children may require different amounts of monitoring.

There are some tools that are necessary for many projects throughout the book—a paper supply, glue, paints, and an art smock.

- **Paper**: There are many places to find scrap paper for the majority of projects. Computer paper, junk mail, and boxes are just three ideas.

- **Glue**: Most projects call for craft, or white, glue. This is a water-based glue that can be thinned for easy application. Fabric glue, which is not water-soluble, holds up outdoors or in projects that will be washed.

- **Paint**: There are many types of paint. A watercolor paint box is an easy, storable, and quality paint application. Poster paint is a tempera paint that comes in powder form or premixed in squeeze bottles. (An empty egg carton works great as a paint box.) Water-based acrylic paint is a vibrant form of paint that can be used on all surfaces. It dries permanently, but when wet is easily cleaned up with water. Make sure your children clean painting tools thoroughly when they are finished painting.

- **Art Smock**: Make sure your child wears a smock or one of your old shirts to protect clothes while working with paints and other messy materials such as clay.

This book should provide an enjoyable, creative experience for both you and your child. Encourage children to create their own versions of each project, using their own ideas. Make the most of a rainy day by creating unique, fabulous crafts and jumping into interesting, thought-provoking activities. Whatever the weather, *Rainy Day Fun* is sure to provide loads of enjoyment!

CHAPTER 1
ART PROJECTS

TAG-TEAM ART

An artist can see a sunset in a line, a face in a circle, or a mountain in a squiggle on a page. What do you see?

WHAT YOU'LL NEED:

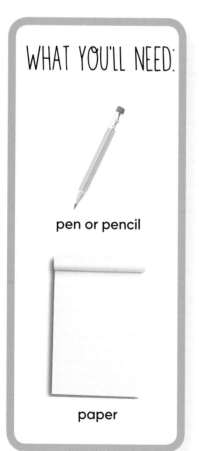

pen or pencil

paper

Art is twice as fun when you share the pencil! The rules are simple. Player 1 draws a line, squiggle, or simple shape on a piece of paper. As soon as you lift your pencil, it's the next player's turn. Player 2 takes the paper and adds another line, squiggle, or shape, trying to turn the art into a picture.

Don't tell the other person what you are trying to draw. That might spoil some of the surprise. What you think is going to be a seagull might turn out to be a sunflower! See how long you can keep adding lines to your artwork. When you decide that your masterpiece is finished, start a new picture.

Some of our favorite playground games originated in other countries. Next time you play Simon Says or Mother, May I, tell your friends that these games came from Ireland!

PAINTING IN OPPOSITES

Every color has an opposite, or complementary, color. Use the opposite color of what's expected and create a surprising world.

WHAT YOU'LL NEED:

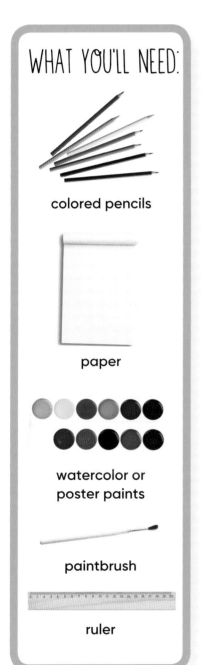

colored pencils

paper

watercolor or poster paints

paintbrush

ruler

Do you know which colors are the primary colors? They are red, blue, and yellow. Which colors are the secondary colors? Mixing the primary colors creates the secondary colors. They are green, orange, and purple. Now that you know which colors are which, draw a color wheel. To create a color wheel, draw a circle on a piece of drawing paper. Use a ruler to divide it into 6 equal "pie" pieces. Label or color in every other "pie" piece as a primary color. To fill in the opposite secondary colors, label the "pie" piece opposite the red section as the secondary color green, the piece opposite the blue as orange, and the piece opposite the yellow as purple.

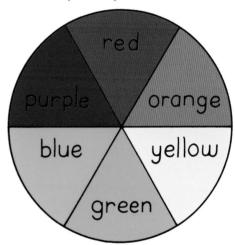

Cover your work surface with newspaper. On a fresh piece of paper, draw a summer scene of a field with flowers and trees, then paint it in opposite colors. Use your color wheel to pick the opposites. For example, your grass will be red, and the sky will be orange with a purple sun. Let the paint dry before you hang your picture.

CRAZY PUTTY DOUGH

With this putty dough, you can make all sorts of silly shapes or magically lift pictures off the funny pages.

WHAT YOU'LL NEED:

$1/3$ cup liquid starch

baking sheet

1 cup craft glue

craft stick or small spoon

newspaper comics

paper

Pour $1/3$ cup liquid starch on a baking sheet. Using a craft stick, slowly stir in 1 cup craft glue. After the mixture starts to clump, let it set for 5 minutes. Dab a small amount of starch on your fingers and knead the mixture. Now you can pull it, roll it, and stretch it—just like putty!

As you experiment with your homemade putty, use the baking sheet as your work surface. (Be careful not to get any putty on the carpet or furniture.)

You can also use the putty to make prints of your favorite comics. Press it on the comic strip, peel it back, and then press the putty on a piece of paper. When you're finished playing with the putty, store it in a small, airtight plastic container.

ANIMAL COMBOS

Mix and match animal features and colors to draw the most unusual zoo in the world.

WHAT YOU'LL NEED:

tracing paper

black felt-tip pen

drawing paper

colored pencils

Find pictures of two different animals that are about the same size. Place a piece of tracing paper over one animal, such as a giraffe, and use a black felt-tip pen to trace the head and neck. Then place the tracing paper over the other animal—a fox, perhaps—and trace the body and legs. You've just created a giraffox!

Place a sheet of drawing paper over your drawing, and trace the giraffox. Using colored pencils, give your giraffox a wild coat. Add feathers, fur, horns, or tails of other creatures to make your animal look even more different.

Use this drawing technique to create all kinds of original animals. Think of combinations to make the most ferocious, the fastest, or the most colorful creature.

Skunks and great horned owls probably wouldn't make a good animal combo. Great horned owls are immune to the skunks' scent and actually find them quite tasty! Someone should tell them to look out, because skunks can spray up to 12 feet!

IRONED COLLAGE

This project creates a stained glass effect, and it looks especially pretty when you hang it in a window.

WHAT YOU'LL NEED:

collage items such as colored tissue paper, doilies, glitter, and tinsel

plastic sandwich bag

aluminum foil

iron and ironing board

needle and thread

Arrange colored tissue paper, doilies, glitter, tinsel, and any other thin, flat items in a design or pattern inside a plastic sandwich bag. You can overlap different colors of tissue paper to create new color combinations, sprinkle glitter to add sparkle, and create flowers with doilies. Seal the bag shut. Then place the bag between two pieces of aluminum foil. With an adult's help, iron the "sandwiched" bag for about 15 seconds. The bag will melt and hold your collage in place. After the collage has cooled, poke a hole in the top center of the bag with a needle. String it with thread to hang it in a window.

Early stained glass artists followed a cartoon pattern (a full-sized preliminary drawing) to cut out the glass pieces. The irregular shapes of the pieces create the beautiful light patterns that we see when the sun shines through a stained glass window.

SAND PAINTINGS

People have made sand paintings for centuries.

WHAT YOU'LL NEED:

cardboard or posterboard

pencil

glue

water

paintbrush

colored sand

To make your own sand painting, you'll need several colors of sand. You can collect sand from nature, or buy it at a crafts store.

Start with a piece of cardboard or posterboard. Set your posterboard on plenty of old newspapers. Use a pencil to draw a picture.

Next, make a mixture of half white glue and half water. Use a paintbrush to paint a thin, even layer of the glue-and-water mixture every place where you want one color of sand. Sprinkle sand over the painted areas. Let dry for a few minutes, then turn your picture over and tap off the extra sand over a trash can.

Repeat the process with the next color sand: Paint glue on all the areas that will be the same color. Sprinkle on the sand, let dry, and tap off. Repeat this process until you've finished your sand painting.

STAINED GLASS PICTURE

Create a picture that looks like stained glass.
It's just as pretty, and it isn't breakable.

WHAT YOU'LL NEED:

construction paper

pencil

food coloring

small squeeze
bottle of
white glue

toothpick

crayons
or
markers

With a pencil, draw a picture on a piece of construction paper. After you've drawn the picture, use lines to divide it into "pieces" like a stained glass window. Add 5 to 10 drops of food coloring to a bottle of glue. Squeeze a line of glue along the lines of the picture to outline each big shape. Use a toothpick to wipe away excess glue. When the glue dries, color in each area with crayons or markers to give your picture a stained glass look.

TOOTHPICK SCULPTURE

You need patience and a steady hand to create these toothpick designs, but the result is well worth the effort.

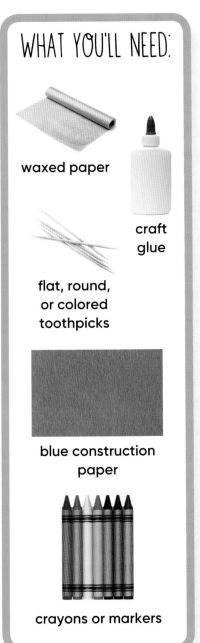

WHAT YOU'LL NEED:

waxed paper

craft glue

flat, round, or colored toothpicks

blue construction paper

crayons or markers

Cover your work surface with a sheet of waxed paper. Glue toothpicks together to make a skeleton shape of a shark. Dip the toothpick ends in glue; then glue each toothpick to the others piece by piece. After you've created the base of the shark, fill in the body with long and broken toothpicks until the shape is rounded. Then add fins and a tail. Let the glue dry.

To make a display stand for your sculpture, fold a piece of blue construction paper in half lengthwise. Draw some waves with crayons or markers. Glue the shark to the paper.

COILED BOWL

This is truly a bowl of a different color, and it becomes extra special when you make it yourself!

WHAT YOU'LL NEED:

assorted colors of polymer clay

waxed paper

scissors

aluminum foil

ovenproof bowl (about the size of a mixing bowl)

craft knife

Using the palms of your hands, roll clay on waxed paper to make 9 to 10 rolls of clay, each about 10 inches long. Then form each clay piece into a circular coil. Cut a circular piece of foil slightly larger than a medium-size ovenproof bowl. Place coiled clay pieces on the foil close together like puzzle pieces. Use your fingers to smooth the surface of the coils until the clay blends together. (Dipping your fingers in water helps to smooth the clay.) Make sure there are no gaps between the pieces. Use a craft knife to trim edges if necessary. Turn the ovenproof bowl upside down, and turn the coiled-clay sheet over onto the bowl. Press the clay sheet around the shape of the bowl. With an adult's help, bake the bowl according to directions on the package of clay. After the clay has cooled, remove foil and bowl from clay.

Ask an adult for help before you begin.

STILL LIFE PICTURE

Bring old wallpaper samples to life by layering different patterns, shapes, and colors on one background.

WHAT YOU'LL NEED:

wallpaper scraps or old wallpaper books

scissors

posterboard

craft glue

Here's a great way to use leftover wallpaper. (If you don't have any wallpaper scraps, you can get old wallpaper books at a home decorating store.) Cut "still life" shapes such as a table, a bowl, and fruit from different patterns of wallpaper scraps. Now set up your "still life" scene on a piece of posterboard. You can leave the posterboard plain or glue a sheet of wallpaper over it to create a wallpapered background for your "still life" scene. Place the wallpaper table on the posterboard background, then put the bowl shape on top of the table, and add the fruit shapes in the bowl. Once you've arranged the pieces, glue them in place.

Not all still life paintings feature groupings of fruit or flowers. Some of the most famous still life pictures were painted by pop artists in the 1960s and feature soup cans and soda pop bottles!

SALT & WATERCOLOR PICTURE

Salt is great on popcorn, but did you know it's also fun to sprinkle it over a wet painting?

WHAT YOU'LL NEED:

pencil

drawing paper

watercolor paints

paintbrush

salt

Cover your work surface with newspaper. Sketch a picture, such as a panda in a forest, on a piece of drawing paper. Paint the drawing using watercolor paint. While the paint is still wet, sprinkle it with salt. Let it dry. The painting will take on a textured look, and the paper may even crinkle and pucker. You can use this painting technique to make textured backgrounds for holiday cards, stationery, and more.

Most people probably think of salt as a food seasoning found on their dinner table, but it is far more than that. Years ago, salt actually served as money. In fact, Roman soldiers were paid with special salt rations. This is where the word "salary" originated!

BULLETIN BOARD DISPLAY

With your very own bulletin board, you always have a place to keep important notes, party invitations, or special photographs.

WHAT YOU'LL NEED:

masking tape

corkboard or bulletin board with a flat wood frame

poster paints and paintbrushes

plastic coffee can lid

scissors

sponge

Cover your work surface with newspaper. Place masking tape around the edges of the bulletin board cork, inside the frame. Paint the frame in a color to match your room. If any paint gets on the cork, wipe it off with a damp paper towel. Let the paint dry.

Cut a small circle from the plastic coffee can lid. To make a stencil, sketch a shape on the plastic circle; make sure the shape is not wider than the corkboard frame. Cut the shape out.

Dip a damp sponge in paint and dab off the excess. Place your stencil on the frame and fill the stencil in by dabbing the sponge straight down onto the surface. Repeat your pattern all around the frame. Let the paint dry.

Here is a stencil you can use.

OPPOSITE ADS

Make 2 or 3 ads for the same pretend product. Then show them to your friends to see which one "sells" your product the best.

WHAT YOU'LL NEED:

drawing paper

colored pencils, markers, or crayons

How would you sell the worst video game, the yuckiest cookies, or the most boring book? How could you eat, much less sell, computer chip cookies or slimy cookies? Advertisements always have a picture or a photo, some writing (called "copy"), and a headline. Invent your own yucky product. Draw a picture and headline for the worst ad, and give your product an awful name. If you'd rather not sell something that's bad, try to sell something that isn't usually for sale. Sell a field trip, honesty, or a dentist appointment.

In the Middle Ages, products were often advertised by town criers. These criers were citizens who were employed by shop owners to shout out the praises of their merchandise. There was hardly any print advertising until the invention of the printing press.

ORIGAMI LEAP FROG

Origami is the Japanese art of folding paper into objects. Turn a piece of paper into a frog and race it across the table.

WHAT YOU'LL NEED:

3x5-inch blank index card

black felt-tip pen

Follow the illustrations to fold the index card.

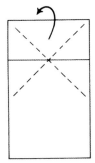 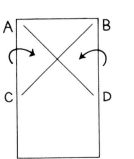 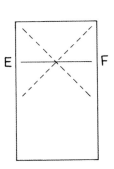

Fold point A to point D. Unfold and repeat with the other corner, folding point B to point C. Fold the top half of the paper back, and then unfold it.

Holding the sides at point E and point F, push them in together toward the center. Press the top half of the paper down, creating a triangle.

Fold the point G corner of the triangle up to point I at the top of the triangle, and form a small triangle. Repeat with the other corner of the large triangle at point H.

Fold the tiny triangles in half, lengthwise. Then fold each side of the index card in about $\frac{1}{4}$ inch.

Fold the bottom end of the index card up $\frac{3}{4}$ inch. Then fold that piece down in half. Turn your frog over, and draw on eyes. Press your finger on the frog's back to make it leap.

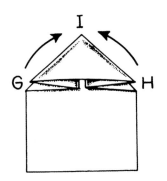

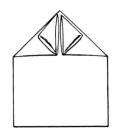  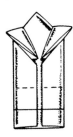

RICE PICTURES

Colored rice gives your picture a grainy texture. Experiment with different dyes such as chalk or even spices.

WHAT YOU'LL NEED:

pastel chalk or spices such as ground mustard, cinnamon, and paprika

cheese grater

craft glue

white rice

paper plates

construction paper

old paintbrush

With an adult's help, grate one color of chalk onto a paper plate using a cheese grater. Repeat with other colors, keeping each one separate. Or place different colors of spices on paper plates. Mix uncooked white rice in with each color.

Next, dilute craft glue with water. Use an old paintbrush to paint a picture on a sheet of construction paper with the diluted glue. Choosing one color of rice, hold the paper plate like a funnel and pour the colored rice over the glue. Let it set, then pour off the excess rice. Repeat the process on another area of the picture using a different color rice.

In eastern India, finger paintings using rice powder mixed with water are painted on walls and floors to accompany harvest and religious festivals. The basic patterns have been handed down for many centuries—as long as rice has been grown in eastern India.

Ask an adult for help before you begin.

PERSONAL POSTCARDS

Instead of writing a letter, why not send a personal "hello" to your friends and relatives with handmade postcards?

WHAT YOU'LL NEED:

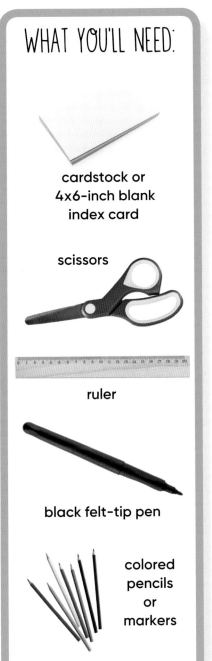

cardstock or 4x6-inch blank index card

scissors

ruler

black felt-tip pen

colored pencils or markers

Cut a 4x6-inch piece from cardstock or use a blank index card. On one side of the cardstock, create the back of a postcard. Using a ruler, draw a straight line down the center of the card to divide one half for the address and the other half for the greeting. On the half for the address (the right side), use a ruler to draw three straight horizontal lines on the lower half of the card. On the front side of the card, create the front of a postcard. Draw anything you'd like. The only limitation is your imagination! Color the picture with colored pencils or markers.

TESSELLATIONS

A tessellation is like a mosaic, using small squares to make a repetitive picture. Try one on your own. It's fun!

WHAT YOU'LL NEED:

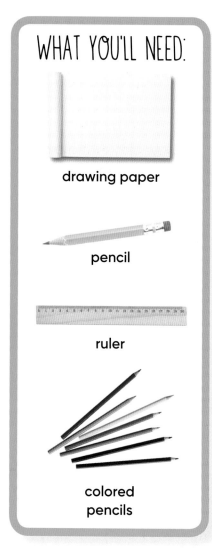

drawing paper

pencil

ruler

colored pencils

Draw a grid of nine squares on a piece of drawing paper. On the left side of one square, draw a curvy line. Repeat that same line on the left side of each square. Now draw a different curvy line at the top of the first square. Then draw the curvy line at the top of each remaining square. Take a look at the squares to see what the shape is starting to look like. Fill in more lines to create a shape, repeating the same line in each square. Each line creates part of the next square's design. When you are done, you should have the same shape in each square. Color your design using colored pencils.

Many of our favorite patchwork patterns were originally designed thousands of years ago by artists working with tile. The floors and walls of some stately Greek and Roman villas were tiled with the same patterns and mosaics that we see in some homes today!

CLAY PENCIL HOLDER

This unique holder keeps all your pens and pencils close at hand and neatly organized.

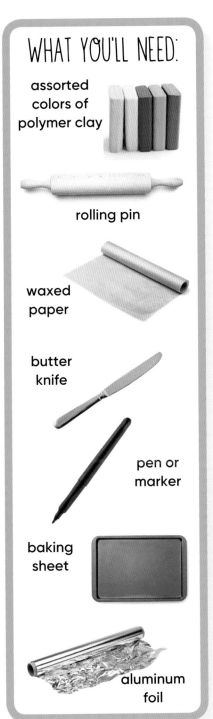

WHAT YOU'LL NEED:

assorted colors of polymer clay

rolling pin

waxed paper

butter knife

pen or marker

baking sheet

aluminum foil

Roll pancakes of red, orange, yellow, green, blue, and purple clay on waxed paper. Stack them on top of each other in order of the colors of the rainbow (red, orange, yellow, green, blue, purple), then cut them into a 1½x7-inch rectangle. (This size will hold about 8 pencils. If you want it to hold more pencils, make the rectangle longer.) Bend the rainbow clay into a big arch with your hands. Using a pen cap, poke a hole in the clay near one end. Make sure the hole is deep enough to hold a pen or pencil. Make 7 more holes, spaced about ¾ inch apart from each other. (If you want more pencils in the holder, make the rectangle longer and poke more holes in it.)

With an adult's help, bake the clay arch according to package directions. Place the rainbow on a baking sheet, then wad up some foil and place it under the arch for support. Once the clay has baked, let it cool and then put your pencils in the holder.

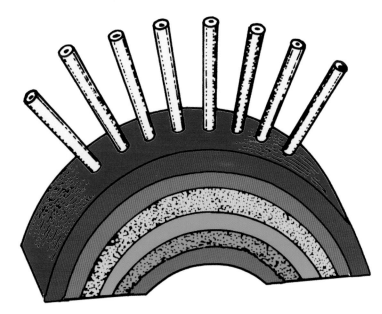

POSITIVE-NEGATIVE CUTOUTS

Yes, you'll have lots of fun. No, you'll never run out of ideas.
You'll want to do this project again and again.

WHAT YOU'LL NEED:

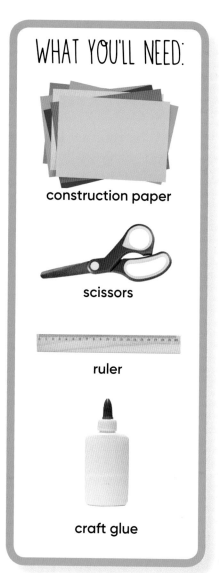

construction paper

scissors

ruler

craft glue

Cut a 4x4-inch square from construction paper. Cut a shape into each side, saving the cut-out pieces. Place the cut square and the cutouts on another piece of brightly colored construction paper. Arrange the cutouts in a mirror image of the square's side shapes. After you've positioned the pieces, glue your design to the construction paper background.

Experiment with all kinds of shapes. You can even glue small cutouts in the center of bigger ones. Or you can tear out the pieces instead of using scissors to cut them. After you've created several cutouts, make them into a collage or frame the finished pieces.

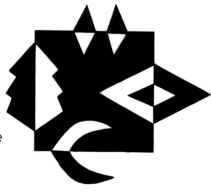

For each positive number, there exists a negative number that is its opposite. For example, the opposite of 12 is -12. When you add any number to its opposite, the answer is always 0, but did you know that 0 is not a positive OR a negative number—it's just 0!

MARBLE PAINTING

You're never boxed in with this unpredictable painting technique. No two designs are ever alike.

WHAT YOU'LL NEED:

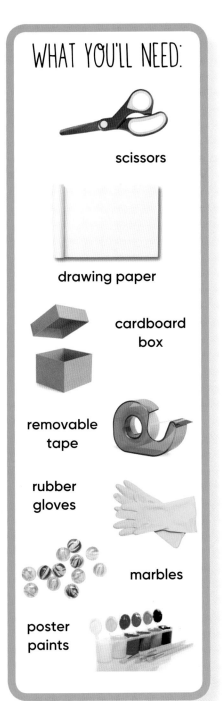

scissors

drawing paper

cardboard box

removable tape

rubber gloves

marbles

poster paints

Cut a piece of drawing paper to fit the bottom of your box. Tape the paper to the bottom of the box with removable tape. Wearing rubber gloves, dip a marble in poster paint. Place the marble on the paper. Now tilt, wiggle, and twirl the box to make designs—the marble is your paintbrush! Let the paint dry. Then use more marbles dipped in other colors to add to your design. Experiment with different colors of paper and paint. Start with red paper and make only white marble tracks. Or try black paper with fluorescent-colored paints. Once all the colors are dry, remove the paper from the box and display your artwork on the wall.

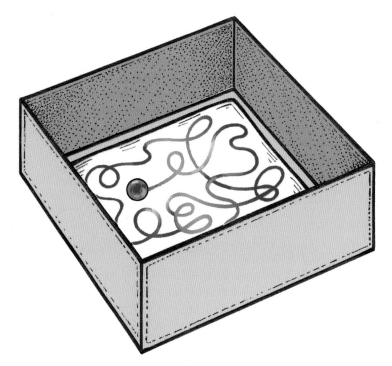

PYRAMID PICTURES

By overlapping several pieces of construction paper, you're building a picture to create depth.

WHAT YOU'LL NEED:

assorted colors of construction paper

scissors

markers

craft glue

Cut a small rectangle from a piece of construction paper. Draw an object or design on it. Cut a slightly larger rectangle from a different color of construction paper. Glue the small rectangle on top of the larger one. Add more detail to your picture. Then cut an even larger rectangle from another color of construction paper. Glue the previous rectangles on top of the bigger rectangle. Draw more designs around your picture. Repeat the process as often as you like to make a pyramid of pictures.

As a variation, you can draw parts of a picture on each piece to create one complete scene. Or, instead of rectangles, cut out octagon shapes. Glue them on top of one another, turning them a bit each time to make your picture into a star.

CRAYON SUN CATCHER

Melted crayons swirl around to become a kaleidoscope of colors, and the bumpy surface makes a wonderful texture.

WHAT YOU'LL NEED:

crayons

handheld pencil sharpener

waxed paper

kitchen or bath towel

iron and ironing board

hot pad or oven mitts

scissors

needle and thread

Twist old crayons in a small handheld pencil sharpener to make shavings. Spread them on a sheet of waxed paper, and place another sheet on top. Cover your "sandwich" with a towel. With an adult's help, iron it until the crayons are melted. Remove the towel, and use a hot pad or oven mitt to smooth over the waxed paper. This will spread the crayons, mixing the colors together. After the wax has cooled, cut the waxed paper into a flower, a star, or any shape you want. To make a hanger, poke a hole through the top of the sun catcher with a needle. String with thread to hang it in your window.

How does a kaleidoscope work? It's all done with mirrors! Mirrors placed in different arrangements produce very different images. A 2-mirror scope makes a single circular design, 3 mirrors make an endless field of pattern, and 4 mirrors make an entire parade of images!

Ask an adult for help before you begin.

BUBBLE PRINTS

Usually when you blow bubbles, they pop and disappear.
Now you can save your bubbles on a piece of paper.

WHAT YOU'LL NEED:

½ cup water

1 teaspoon dish soap

food coloring

plastic cup

baking sheet

plastic drinking straw

white drawing paper

markers

Mix ½ cup water, 1 teaspoon dish soap, and a few drops of food coloring in a plastic cup. Place the plastic cup on a baking sheet. Place the straw in the cup, and blow bubbles through the straw until they spill all over the baking sheet. Make sure you don't suck any bubbles into your mouth! Remove the cup and place a piece of paper on top of the bubbles. Lift the paper off. The colored bubbles will create a light design on the paper. Let it dry, then draw in a picture or outline shapes in the design. Use this bubble-printed paper as wrapping paper, book covers, or stationery.

CARTOON CAPER

You don't need a TV to see cartoons whenever you want!

WHAT YOU'LL NEED:

sheet of notebook paper cut into long strips

pencil

Fold a strip of paper in half. On the bottom flap, draw a cartoon that shows half of a simple action—for example, a person sitting in a chair. On the top flap, show the other half of the action; for example, a person standing in front of a chair (Picture 1). Now roll the upper flap tightly around a pencil to give it a strong curl (Picture 2).

Hold the upper corner flat against the table, and move the pencil rapidly up and down as shown to make the flap unroll and roll up again (Picture 3). If you do it fast enough, it looks like a cartoon of a person sitting and standing over and over again. You can draw anything you like: a dog running, a face smiling, a ball bouncing, and so on. How many cartoon books can you create?

Picture 1

Picture 2

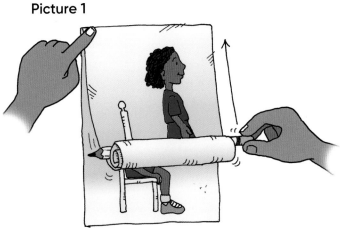

Picture 3

THUMMIES

With your thumbprint as a starting point, you can come up with all sorts of art creations.

WHAT YOU'LL NEED:

water-based ink
stamp pad

drawing paper

fine-point
felt-tip pen

Press your thumb on an ink pad, then press it on a piece of paper. With a fine-point felt-tip pen, add details to your thumbprint to create an animal, a person, or a silly character. Draw ears, whiskers, and a tail to make a cat, or add spots, legs, and antennae to make a ladybug. There are many fun creations you can make with thummies.

Try using your pinky or index finger for prints in different sizes and shapes. Or press four or five thummies in a row to make a caterpillar. Use thummies to decorate greeting cards and stationery or to illustrate a story.

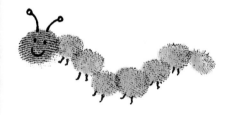

PAPIER-MÂCHÉ MASK

Build an original mask out of newspaper strips, and then display your artwork on the wall.

WHAT YOU'LL NEED:

newspaper cut into 1x4-inch strips

scissors or craft knife

stapler and staples

masking tape

flour and water (for paste)

acrylic or poster paints and paintbrush

acrylic sealer (optional)

Cover your work surface with newspaper. Fold several sheets of newspaper into long bands. Using the illustration as a guide, make a mask frame (an oval half) with bands of newspaper stapled together.

Mask frame

Mix flour and water together to make a paste. (Use 1 cup of flour for each cup of water.) Blend until the paste is smooth. Dip a strip of newspaper in the paste. Rub the strip between your fingers to remove any extra paste. Put the strip over the mask frame and smooth it in place. Repeat until the mask is covered with 4 or 5 layers of strips. To add more dimension to

your mask, tape on projections before you add the last layer of newspaper strips. Use paper rolls or cones for horns, ears, and a nose. Let the mask dry overnight.

With an adult's help, cut out the eyes and mouth. Paint the mask and let it dry completely. To make your mask shiny, apply a coat of acrylic sealer.

MAKE ENVELOPES

Don't throw away all those printed materials that add up around the house. Here's a better idea!

WHAT YOU'LL NEED:

variety of printed materials (such as maps, placemats, brochures, etc.)

scissors

ruler

clear tape

If the printed document is much larger than an average sheet of paper, cut it down into a rectangle shape (longer on one side, shorter on the other). A sheet of notebook paper (8½x11 inches) is a good size to practice with.

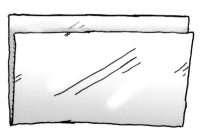

Picture 1

Pick which side you want to be on the outside of your envelope. Lay that side facedown, and position the paper so that the longer side goes from left to right. Fold up the bottom 4 inches of the paper and crease well (Picture 1). Then fold the sides over about half an inch, using tape to seal them in place (Picture 2). After you've written a letter and put it inside,

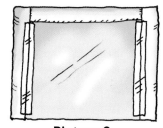

Picture 2

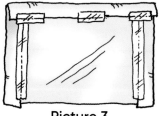

Picture 3

close and seal the remaining flap (Picture 3). Put the postage, the address you're sending the letter to, and your return address on the other side of the envelope. Use address labels if your envelope is too dark to read easily or is difficult to write on.

NAME ART

Turn your name into a work of art!

WHAT YOU'LL NEED:

pencil

paper

crayons

Print your first name in large, neat letters. Now take a long look at them. What does the shape of each letter remind you of? A small letter b might be a baseball with a bat standing next to it. A capital S might be a snake or a pair of monkey arms. Try turning each letter into an object or animal so that your name looks like the things that interest you.

Can you do the same thing with your last name? What about other people's names?

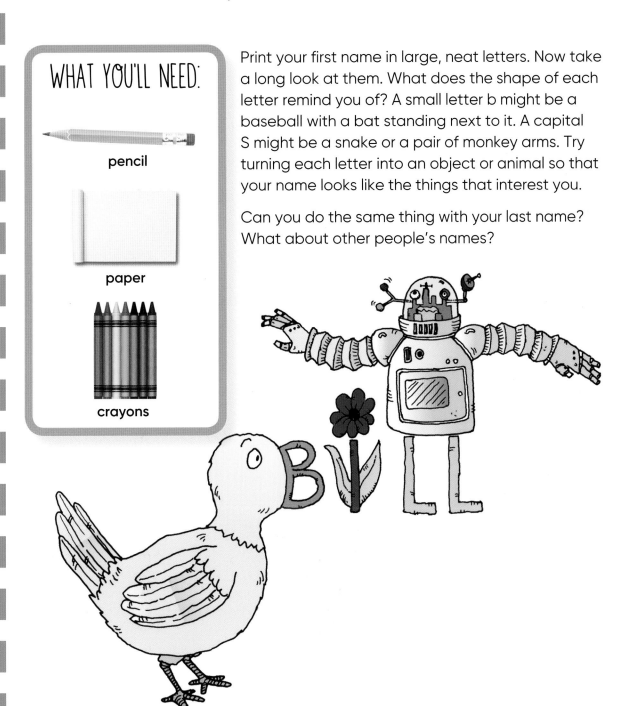

CHALK IT

It's incredible how one piece of pastel chalk creates two different colors when used on wet paper and then on dry paper.

WHAT YOU'LL NEED:

sponge

construction paper

pastel chalk

hairspray
(optional)

Lightly dab a moist sponge on one half of a sheet of construction paper to dampen it. Draw a design on both the wet and dry halves of the paper with pastel chalks. Make a squiggle picture by drawing a continuous curvy line all around the paper. Add more squiggles, and color in the spaces. Now compare the colors on the wet and dry surfaces of the paper. When the paper dries, have an adult seal the picture with a fine mist of hairspray.

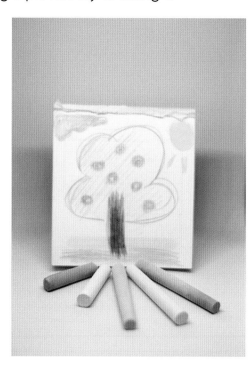

Chalk isn't just for use on the blackboard! Putty, plaster, cement, and building stones are all made with chalk. In fact, farmers will sometimes use chalk to improve poor soils with high clay content.

EMBOSSING PAPER

This is a double treat, since collecting your supplies is as much fun as making the embossed paper itself.

WHAT YOU'LL NEED:

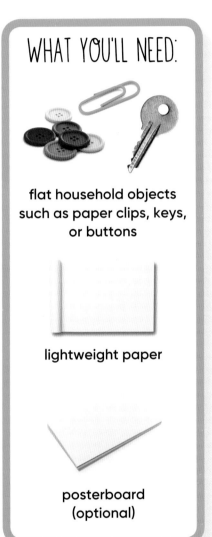

flat household objects such as paper clips, keys, or buttons

lightweight paper

posterboard (optional)

Look for flat objects, such as paper clips and keys, around your house. Place a piece of lightweight paper over a paper clip and rub over the paper with your finger.

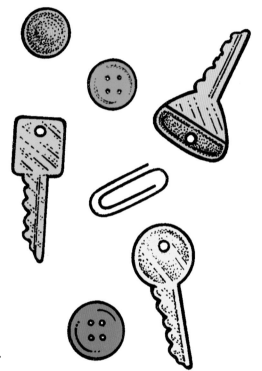

Lift the paper, and notice the textured shape on the paper. You've just created embossed paper.

To make embossed designs, rub over an object and move it from place to place under a piece of paper. Use a key to make the petals of a flower. Or cut a wavy edge on a strip of posterboard, and use it to make an embossed line at the top and bottom of your paper. It's a pretty decoration for stationery.

SHIRT PAINTING

Housepaint turns a T-shirt into something cool—especially if you use colors found in your very own home.

WHAT YOU'LL NEED:

white T-shirt

large plastic bag

sponges

scissors

water-based housepaint

clean foam meat tray

scrap paper

When housepaint gets on clothes, it won't come off. Here's how you can use that fact to your advantage. Place a T-shirt over spread-out newspaper. Put a large plastic bag inside the shirt, between the back and front. To paint your shirt, make some printing stamps using sponges. For instance, you might cut the sponges in the shape of a star, crescent moon, and sun. Put some housepaint in a clean foam tray and dip a damp sponge in the paint. Dab off the excess paint on scrap paper. Now print your design on the shirt. Let the paint dry completely before you wear or wash the shirt.

FOIL PRINTMAKING

This printing technique allows you to transfer a picture piece by piece.

WHAT YOU'LL NEED:

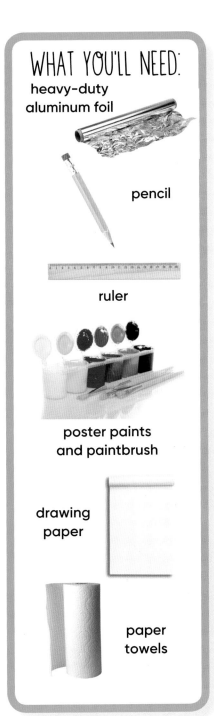

heavy-duty
aluminum foil

pencil

ruler

poster paints
and paintbrush

drawing
paper

paper
towels

Cover your work surface with newspaper. Draw a square on a sheet of foil. Make the square slightly smaller than the paper sheet you will print on. (Measure with a ruler to make sure.) Then draw a picture in the foil square. Select one color of paint, and paint in the parts of the picture using that color. Then place a sheet of paper over the foil print, and press. Carefully peel off the paper, and let the paint dry. Use a damp paper towel to wipe off the old color from the foil. Now select a different color, and paint in another area of the picture. Reprint it on the paper as before. Continue reprinting the paper until you use all your colors and your picture is complete.

According to the Aluminum Association, nearly 75 percent of all the aluminum produced in the United States is still in use today thanks to recycling. Aluminum can be recycled over and over again without any loss of quality.

MODELING CLAY DOUGH

It's amazing how many interesting shapes you can make with this colorful and fun clay dough.

WHAT YOU'LL NEED:

1 cup flour

$\frac{1}{2}$ cup salt

1 tablespoon vegetable oil

1 cup water

bowl

waxed paper

Mix 1 cup flour, $\frac{1}{2}$ cup salt, 1 tablespoon vegetable oil, and 1 cup water together in a big bowl until the mixture becomes doughlike. Place a sheet of waxed paper on your work surface, and sprinkle it with some flour. Knead the clay dough into a ball on the floured waxed paper. Divide the ball into separate lumps of clay, and add some food coloring to each. Knead each lump well again. Now you can sculpt the clay dough into any shape you want. When you're done sculpting, you can leave your clay creations out to air dry, or store the clay in separate plastic bags or airtight containers. Keep them in the refrigerator until the next time you play.

When heated, clay becomes hard and holds its shape.
Sun-dried bricks made of clay are among the most ancient building materials. In some parts of the world, clay has been discovered that is over 5,000 years old!

BIG BRUSH ART

All the best artists know that sometimes an unusual paintbrush creates the most remarkable picture.

WHAT YOU'LL NEED:

large cardboard box

scissors

large paintbrush or foam brush

poster paints

With an adult's help, cut out a large panel of cardboard from a cardboard box. Cover your work area with newspaper. Paint a painting on your cardboard "canvas" using a large paintbrush and poster paint. Illustrate something big, such as a skyscraper, the Grand Canyon, or a Ferris wheel. You can also paint something that is small on a large scale. Try filling the whole space with one autumn leaf or a bouquet of sunflowers.

One of tallest buildings in the United States is the Willis Tower, located in Chicago, Illinois. It is 1,450 feet tall from the ground to the top of its roof. In other words, it would take approximately 325 children, with an average height of 54 inches, standing end to end, to reach the top!

ART IN PIECES

One picture is worth 1,000 giggles when you try drawing a picture in 9 separate sections.

WHAT YOU'LL NEED:

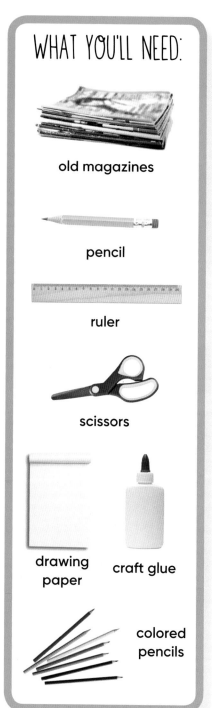

old magazines

pencil

ruler

scissors

drawing paper

craft glue

colored pencils

Find a picture you like in a magazine. Draw a large square around it, then divide it into 9 equal squares. Cut out the small squares. On a piece of drawing paper, draw the picture from one of the cut squares; you can even turn the square upside down to concentrate on the lines. As you draw, concentrate on the spacing of the lines rather than the outline. Repeat this drawing technique for each square.

After you're done drawing, cut out the squares, reassemble your picture on a piece of paper, and glue the squares in place. Color in your picture.

Another idea is to fill in your square pieces using different coloring tools before you put them together. Color some in with crayon, chalk, or even acrylic or watercolor paints.

BATHTUB ART

When you're done with one foamy picture, lightly wipe your hand over the surface and you have a new canvas.

WHAT YOU'LL NEED:

shaving cream or nondairy whipped cream

design tools such as a comb, washcloth, or sponge

baking sheet (optional)

food coloring

Here's a fun project to do while you are in the bathtub. Cover a side wall of the tub with a big handful of shaving cream or nondairy whipped cream. Use your fingers, a comb, a washcloth, or a sponge to draw a picture in the shaving cream. If you want to make a different picture, wipe your hand over the surface of the shaving cream and start all over again. When you are done creating your bathtub art, make sure you rinse off the shaving cream from the bathtub wall.

If you are not in a bathtub, use a baking sheet as your canvas. Place a handful of shaving cream or nondairy whipped cream on the sheet. Add a drop of food coloring to the cream and blend together. Now you're ready to create some fun art.

Did you know that bathtubs with hulls built around them race down the mighty, legendary Yukon River from Whitehorse to Dawson City, Yukon? These tubs cover a span of 427 miles in just 2 days! You can race, too. All you need is a vessel and nerves of steel!

QUILT PICTURE

This looks like an old-fashioned quilt, but there's no sewing needed, and it takes less time than the real thing.

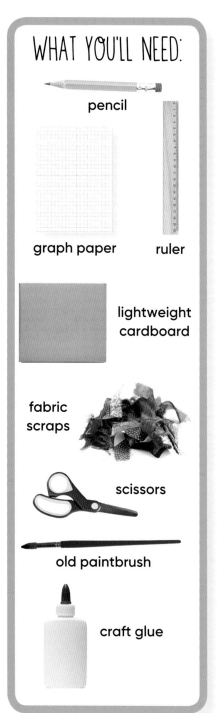
Practice drawing a quilt design on a piece of graph paper. (Quilt designs are often made of interlocking shapes, such as squares, triangles, or even octagons.) Use a ruler to help you draw the triangles and squares of the quilt pattern. Then measure the exact size of the triangles and squares in the design and cut them from cardboard to make the pattern pieces. Place each pattern piece on a fabric scrap and trace around it. Cut out the fabric pieces. Use an old paintbrush to coat the back of each piece with glue. Following the quilt design you drew on graph paper, glue the fabric on the cardboard. After it's dry, trim the cardboard and frame your quilt picture.

STRING ART

This project has a three-dimensional feeling. It looks as if the objects you form are actually leaping off the background.

WHAT YOU'LL NEED:

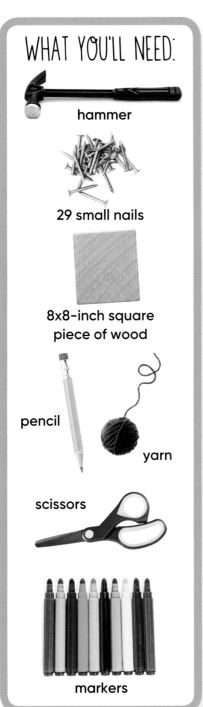

hammer

29 small nails

8x8-inch square piece of wood

pencil

yarn

scissors

markers

Have an adult hammer the nails into the wood base following the placement shown in the illustrations to make a butterfly and flower. Following the illustrations, pencil in a number next to each nail. This will be your guide when you start to string the design.

To string the butterfly, tie one end of the yarn to nail 1. Then string the yarn from nail 1 to nail 20, then bring the yarn back up to nail 2 and down to nail 19. Continue stringing the yarn using the illustration as your guide. Once you're finished, tie the yarn to nail 11. Trim off excess yarn.

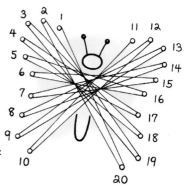

To make the flower, tie one end of the yarn to nail 1. Then string the yarn from nail 1 to nail 5, nail 5 to nail 9, and nail 9 to nail 4. Continue stringing, using the illustration as your guide. When you come back to nail 1, tie the yarn to the nail. Trim off excess yarn.

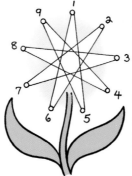

After you've finished stringing, use markers to draw on a stem and leaves for the flower and a head, body, and antennae for the butterfly.

Ask an adult for help before you begin.

THE NEWEST STATE

Invent a state that includes all your favorite things—skiing, sailing, amusement park cities, and even towns that sell nothing but ice cream.

WHAT YOU'LL NEED:

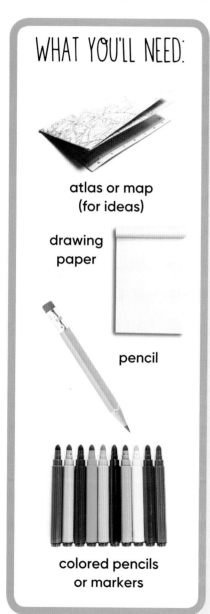

atlas or map
(for ideas)

drawing
paper

pencil

colored pencils
or markers

In order to add the next state to the union, you need to invent it. Look through an atlas to find a state shape you want to copy. Draw the shape on a piece of paper, and make a map of your new state. Name the state and add geographical features. Draw mountains, lakes, shorelines, cities, and the state capital. Color in your new state. Then draw the state flag, seal, and flower.

Now create another state. This time make it as silly and illogical as possible. The state motto can be "We live to ski" or "Fast-food kingdom." Think of city names to go with the state theme.

WEAVE A PLATE

Jazz up this wall hanging with all sorts of trim—some rough, some smooth, some shiny, and even some unexpected, such as wire.

WHAT YOU'LL NEED:

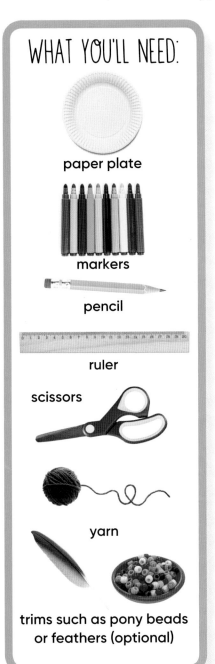

paper plate

markers

pencil

ruler

scissors

yarn

trims such as pony beads or feathers (optional)

Draw a small design in the center of the paper plate with markers. Use a pencil to lightly mark 3-inch increments around the edge of the plate to indicate spacing. Starting about $\frac{1}{2}$ inch from the outer edge of the plate at each of the pencil marks, cut a $2\frac{1}{2}$-inch slit toward the center of the plate. Make sure you don't cut into your center design.

Weave pieces of colorful yarn through the slits. Change colors by tying one color to another. As you weave the yarn, thread on beads or tie in feathers. When you're done weaving the yarn, knot it in back and cut off excess yarn.

MOTHER MOOSE ILLUSTRATED

Change the key words of old nursery rhymes or your favorite story to make a silly poem. Then draw pictures to match your new story.

WHAT YOU'LL NEED:

drawing paper

scissors

colored pencils or markers

construction paper

hole punch

yarn

Cut several sheets of drawing paper in half, depending on how many pages you want your book to be. Write a silly story on a page, and draw matching illustrations. For example, instead of Mary having a little lamb, she can have a giant ham. Make yourself, your family, or your friends the characters in the story.

Rewrite and illustrate several stories for your Mother Moose story book. If you want, add a table of contents and a dedication page.

After you've finished the inside pages, bind your new book. To make the front and back covers,

Becky had a giant ham. It tastes as bad as liver, and everywhere that Becky went the liver went there with her.

fold a sheet of construction paper in half and punch 4 holes near the fold. Decorate the front cover. Then punch 4 holes in each page, making sure they line up with the holes on the covers. Place the pages inside the covers. Cut a piece of yarn, thread it through the holes, and tie it in a bow.

LETTER DESIGNS

Use your imagination to make your own personalized nameplate for your bedroom door or create a fun alphabet game.

WHAT YOU'LL NEED:

drawing paper

colored pencils or markers

scissors

cardboard

ruler

hole punch

craft glue

yarn

On a piece of drawing paper, draw an object in the shape of its first letter. For example, the word snake starts with an s. Draw a snake in an s shape and then write out the rest of the letters in the word. Color in your letter design. Try making a poster of all the letters in the alphabet with letter designs.

To make a nameplate, cut one 3x8-inch rectangle from a piece of paper and one from cardboard. Draw an object in the shape of each letter in your name on the paper. Then color in each letter design. Glue the paper on the cardboard. Then, punch a hole in the top two corners of the nameplate. String it with a piece of yarn to hang it up on your door.

3-D PICTURE

Outline a simple picture with colorful paper to make it a three-dimensional work of art.

WHAT YOU'LL NEED:

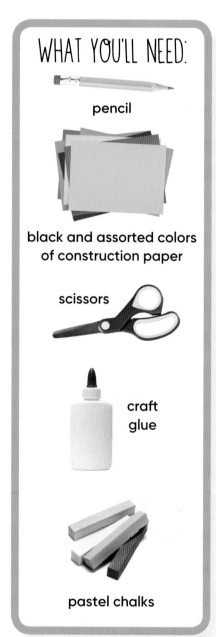

pencil

black and assorted colors of construction paper

scissors

craft glue

pastel chalks

Draw a car on a piece of black construction paper. Then cut ¾-inch-wide strips from bright-colored construction paper to outline the wheels, doors, and hood of the car. If your car is winding down a country road, outline a tree and a fence. Put a line of glue around each item and stand the paper up in the glue to create the outlines. Bend the paper to match each part of the outline. Outline the whole car in stand-up paper. Use pastel chalks when you are finished to add more color to your picture.

You can also make great Christmas tree ornaments using this technique! After you've outlined your ornament shape, cut it out. Then outline the same design on the other side.

CHAPTER 2
CRAFT ACTIVITIES

PAPERCOPTERS

These paper helicopters spin just like the real thing!

WHAT YOU'LL NEED:

strips of heavy
paper or cardboard
(1x10 inches)

small paper clips

markers or crayons

Fold a 1x10-inch strip of paper in half (Picture 1). Fold the ends down about 2 inches, but don't fold them straight down. Instead, fold them at a slight angle (Picture 2). Next, push a paper clip onto the bottom, and fold the wings out (Picture 3). Decorate your papercopter with markers or crayons. Holding your papercopter by the paper clip, throw it into the air and watch it spin (Picture 4)!

Experiment. What happens if you add more paper clips to the bottom? Or if you use a longer strip of paper to make your papercopter? Or if you fold the wings at more (or less) of an angle?

Picture 1

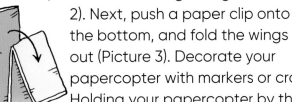

Picture 2

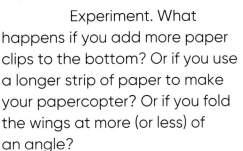

Picture 3

Picture 4

APPLEHEAD DOLLS

These charming, old-fashioned dolls—made from small apples—look like wise old men and women.

WHAT YOU'LL NEED:

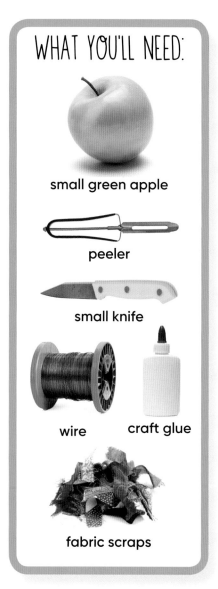

small green apple

peeler

small knife

wire

craft glue

fabric scraps

Small, unripe apples work best for this project, so if you know someone with an apple tree, ask them for some windfallen green apples. Peel the apple, then have an adult help you carve a face in it with a small knife. When you're carving, think of how a real face is shaped. The nose and cheeks stick out, while the eyes are set in, so carve away the front of the apple but leave lumps sticking out for the nose and cheeks. Make exaggerated features, as they will shrink in the drying process. Put the apple in a warm place to dry. This will take a week or more.

When the apple head is dry, bend wire into the shape of a body, with a long neck to stick into the apple head. Dress the doll with clothing cut from fabric scraps and glued on.

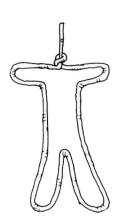

Ask an adult for help before you begin.

BEADS & BAUBLES

Turn common household items into fashionable jewelry. Just a few items are all you need to make a special necklace for a friend.

WHAT YOU'LL NEED:

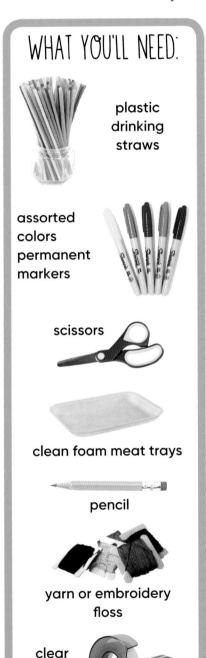

plastic drinking straws

assorted colors permanent markers

scissors

clean foam meat trays

pencil

yarn or embroidery floss

clear tape

Color several drinking straws with permanent markers. Cut them into ¼-, ½-, and 1-inch lengths. Cut a few fun shapes from clean foam meat trays. Decorate the shapes with markers, then punch a hole in the center of each foam bead using the tip of a pencil. String the straws and foam beads on colored yarn or embroidery floss. (Putting a bit of tape around one end of the yarn makes it easier to string.) Tie the ends of the yarn or floss together in a bow.

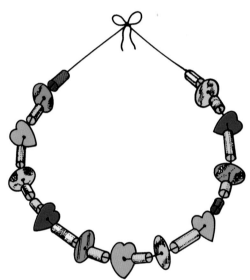

Although the world boasts some incredible treasures, nothing compares with the British Crown Jewels, on display at the Tower of London. These jewels of gold, silver, platinum, diamonds, sapphires, rubies, emeralds, pearls, and more have all been worn and used by the kings and queens of England.

MYSTERY BOXES

*Challenge your friends to discover—by touch only—
what lies in your mystery boxes!*

WHAT YOU'LL NEED:

shoe box

tape

scissors

paper or fabric

markers

nature objects

index cards

For each mystery box, tape the lid onto a shoe box and cut a hole in one end large enough to put your hand through. Cover the hole with paper. Cut 8 slits in the paper in a star shape, so that you can put your hand through but the hole will still be covered. Alternately, instead of paper, you could hang a small piece of fabric inside the box to cover the hole by forming a curtain. Then decorate the box with markers.

Now put a mystery object inside the box. Remember that your friends trust you, so only use objects that won't harm them or make them feel bad in any way. Try shells, rocks, driftwood, leaves, twigs, or cones. Make up a riddle or a poem to go with each object. Write it on a card and put it on the box.

Let your friends put a hand through the hole and try to guess what the object is. After everyone has made a guess, let someone take the object out for all to see.

A box without hinges, key or lid
Yet golden treasure inside is hid...

Guess what?

ART GUM PRINTER

*Make your own rubber stamp from an art gum eraser.
Use it to create different geometric patterns on everything
from stationery to gift boxes.*

WHAT YOU'LL NEED:

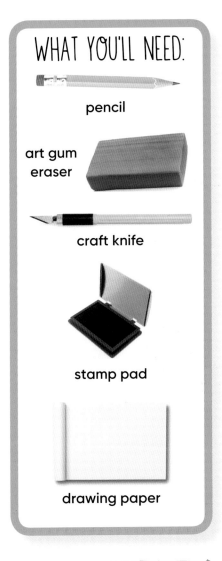

pencil

art gum
eraser

craft knife

stamp pad

drawing paper

Ask an adult for
help before
you begin.

Lightly draw a simple design on one side of an art gum eraser. To make the raised part of your design, have an adult help you use a craft knife to carve out whichever parts you don't want to print.

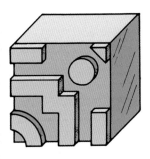

Press the carved side of the eraser down on a stamp pad, then position the eraser on a piece of paper and press down firmly to print your design. Stamp it in repeated patterns, re-inking it every 1 or 2 prints. Be sure to wash the eraser when you change ink colors and when you're done using it.

If you'd like, you may make your eraser into a personal stamp for yourself. Instead of carving out a geometric design, carve out your initials on the eraser. (If you choose to carve letters, make sure they are the mirror image of the real letters so they will print the correct way.) Then use the printer to sign special papers with your "mark."

POPCORN FRAME

The next time you make popcorn, save some for this fun frame!

WHAT YOU'LL NEED:

popped popcorn
(air-popped or plain
microwave varieties
work best)

small self-standing
picture frame (matte)

craft glue

colored pebbles
or marbles

Be sure to let the popcorn cool before starting this project. Don't put butter or salt on it, either. First, glue a layer of popcorn around the edge of the frame. Let the glue dry, then glue some pebbles, marbles, or any other kind of colorful decorations on the frame wherever you want. Let the glue dry again, then fill in any remaining gaps with more popcorn.

Throughout history, people from many cultures have enjoyed popcorn. The first people known to have used popcorn were the American Indians. Not only did they eat it (as early as 400 B.C.), they also used it for necklaces and ceremonial headdresses.

ALPHABET ART

Spell out the objects in your picture with pasta letters.
This art form is called word graphs and it's F-U-N.

WHAT YOU'LL NEED:

alphabet pasta

craft glue

drawing or construction paper

markers

Word graphs use words to draw an outline of an object. For example, in the illustration below, the words "sun" and "shine" form a sun's shape. The word "sun" is used to outline the round part of the sun, and the word "shine" is used to outline the sun's rays. Gather letters from alphabet pasta to make your picture with words. (If you don't have any alphabet pasta, you can still make a word graph— just draw the letters.) Glue the alphabet pasta to a piece of paper to make your picture. Fill in any missing letters or add more details with markers.

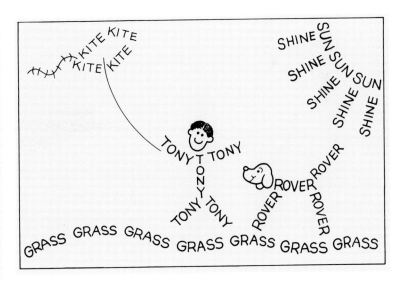

POP-UP GREETING CARD

Give a little extra lift to your message with a special greeting card that springs to life.

WHAT YOU'LL NEED:

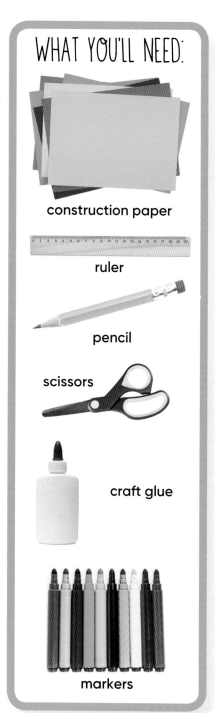

construction paper

ruler

pencil

scissors

craft glue

markers

Fold a piece of construction paper in half. Halfway down the fold, make 2 pencil marks about 2 inches apart. At each mark, cut a slit through the fold 1 inch into the paper.

Fold the cut flap back and forth several times to crease it well. Bring the flap back to center. Unfold the page almost completely, and gently push the flap back toward the open ends. You should have a rectangle that pops out of the paper.

Draw a shape or design for your greeting card on another piece of construction paper. Cut it out, and glue it to the front of the pop-out rectangle. Fold another piece of construction paper in half. Trim the pop-up paper so that it is slightly smaller than the second piece of paper. Glue the back of the pop-up paper to the inside of the larger paper. Decorate the front of your greeting card, and write a message inside.

If you want to make your pop-up cards into a pop-up gift book, repeat steps 1 and 2 to make several pop-up pages. Then draw and cut out the items for a story from construction paper. Glue those shapes on the pop-out rectangles. Glue the back of one page to the front of another. Repeat this until all the pages are glued together. To make a cover, fold another piece of construction paper in half. Glue the first and last pages inside the cover. Decorate the cover.

CHARACTER COLLAGE

Create a family of silly characters using some old magazines, scissors, glue, and your imagination.

WHAT YOU'LL NEED:

old clothing catalogs or magazines

scissors

craft glue

construction paper

Look through old clothing catalogs or magazines. Cut out different heads, hairdos, arms, hands, bodies, clothes, legs, and shoes. Now paste the different parts together on a piece of construction paper to make a mixed-up, new character. Be creative—paste a great big hat on a small head and tiny arms on a big body. Make a whole family of characters and give them a silly family name. You can even paste together parts of objects to make an alien character. For example, the alien could have a car-tire head, gift-box body, feather arms, and key legs.

Animation artists work hard to create films featuring your favorite cartoon characters. Over 4,000 storyboard drawings are created as the blueprint for the action and dialogue of just one typical animated film! Each drawing is usually revised many times while the film is being made.

TOOTHPICK DOLLS

These tiny people can keep you company wherever you go.
Slip them into your pocket, notebook, or schoolbag.

WHAT YOU'LL NEED:

5 toothpicks

ruler

scissors

craft glue

embroidery floss

With an adult's help, cut off $1\frac{1}{4}$ inches from one end of 1 toothpick. This is the body. For the legs, cut off $\frac{5}{8}$ inch from one end of 2 toothpicks. To make the arms, cut off $1\frac{3}{4}$ inches from one end of the remaining 2 toothpicks. Throw away toothpick scraps.

Glue one leg to each side of the toothpick body. Let the glue set. Apply a drop of glue to the side of one leg near the top, and place the end of the embroidery floss on the glue. Wrap the floss around both toothpicks until you get about halfway down, then continue to wrap the floss around just one of the toothpicks, working your way all the way to the bottom. Trim the floss and glue the end in place. For the second leg, place a dab of glue just where the floss ended, then place another

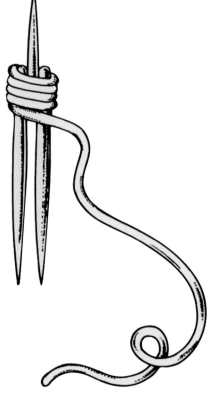

TOOTHPICK DOLLS

piece of floss on the glue and wrap it around the toothpick until you get to the bottom. Trim the floss and glue the end in place.

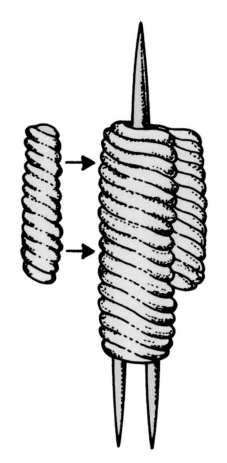

Wrap each toothpick arm with floss, then glue the arms to the sides of the wrapped body (as shown in picture to right). To make the shoulders, add a dot of glue to the toothpick body just above the floss. Place the end of the floss on the glue, and wrap it down around the body to the tops of the arms (about 6 or 7 times). Trim the floss. Glue the end in back.

Make the head by wrapping floss into a ball around the top of the toothpick body. Trim the floss, and glue the end in back. To make the hair, cut several strands of floss. Hold the strands together, and glue them to the top of the doll's head. Trim excess floss.

Ask an adult for help before you begin.

FRUIT PEEL FLOWERS

Try making these unusual Victorian flower decorations.

WHAT YOU'LL NEED:

peels from citrus fruits

spoon

scissors

cookie sheet

candy box

black paper or cloth

strong glue

Back in Victorian days, artificial flowers were often made from paper or feathers, and sometimes even from the peels of oranges, lemons, and grapefruit. To make these flowers, first peel some oranges or other citrus fruits. Use the edge of a spoon to carefully scrape away the white part of the peel until you see fine lines close to the outer, colored part. Rinse and dry the peels; use scissors to cut into the shapes of flower petals and leaves. With help from an adult, spread them out on a cookie sheet and dry in a warm oven (no hotter than 150°F). Don't let them overdry, or they will be brittle. When they are dry they will curl into natural petal shapes.

Next, line an empty candy box with black paper or cloth. Use strong glue to glue the petals into flower shapes on the black background. You can use small seeds from oranges or lemons for the flower centers.

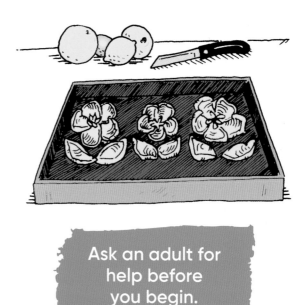

Ask an adult for help before you begin.

BACKSEAT TOTE

When you're in the back of the car, it's easy to lose things under the seat or between the cushions. Make this travel tote to keep your stuff in one place.

WHAT YOU'LL NEED:

1 pair old pants with beltloops

2 feet of rope (or cord or heavy string)

scissors

needle and thread (or sewing machine)

fabric paint or permanent markers (optional)

Ask an adult for help before you begin.

Cut the legs off the pants (Picture 1). With a sewing machine or needle and thread, sew the legs of the pants shut (Picture 2). Tie one end of the rope to a belt loop on the left side of the pants. Tie the other end of the rope to a belt loop on the right side of the pants (Picture 3). Decorate the tote with fabric paint or markers. Hook the rope over the back of the head-rest of the driver's seat or passenger seat (Picture 4). Use this travel tote to hold books, magazines, notepads, snacks, or whatever you want. The pants pockets are perfect for small items such as coins and pens. You can even take your travel tote with you as a carryall.

Picture 1

Picture 2

Picture 3

Picture 4

POP-ME THANK YOU

Burst out with a big "thanks" to someone you love.

WHAT YOU'LL NEED:

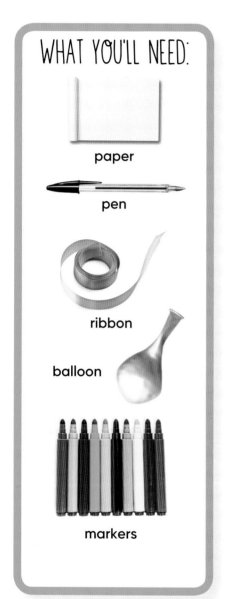

paper

pen

ribbon

balloon

markers

On a small piece of paper, write a thank-you message to the person you want to thank. Roll the paper into a scroll and tie it with a bit of ribbon. Carefully insert the scroll into an uninflated balloon. Blow up the balloon, tie it off, and tie curling ribbon to the end of it. Write "Pop Me" in big letters on the balloon with a marker, deliver the balloon to the person you want to thank, and wait for the bang!

Around the world, people say "thank you" in many different ways. In Japan, when a gift is given, people are sure to say thanks with a return gift called an O-kaeshi. The value of this "thank-you" gift is usually about half the value of the giver's gift.

UP PERISCOPE!

Pretend you're on a submarine with this milk-carton periscope. You can look through the window or around corners, and nobody will know you're there!

WHAT YOU'LL NEED:

- empty 1-quart milk carton (clean and dry)
- scissors
- 2 small mirrors (pocket mirrors or makeup mirrors)
- clear tape

Ask an adult for help before you begin.

Cut a hole on one side of the milk carton near the bottom (Picture 1). The hole should be almost as wide as the carton and 2 inches tall. Cut another hole in the milk carton, this time on the opposite side near the top (Picture 2).

Make it the same size as the first hole. The next part is a little tricky: Tape 2 mirrors inside the milk carton with the mirrored sides facing each other, one at the top, and one at the bottom (Picture 3).

Angle them as shown in the picture. By looking in through the bottom hole of the periscope, you will see through both mirrors and out the top.

Picture 1

Picture 2

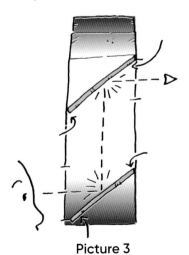

Picture 3

GOD'S EYE

Make your own god's eye by weaving a design with colorful yarn on two crossed sticks.

WHAT YOU'LL NEED:

2 sticks the same size (cotton swabs, pencils, or ice-cream sticks will work)

yarn or string (several colors look prettiest)

Place 2 sticks together to form an X. This is the frame for your god's eye. Tie one end of a piece of yarn around the center of the crossed sticks to hold them together. Make the knot tight so the sticks aren't loose (Picture 1).

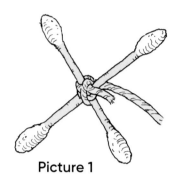

Picture 1

Picture 2

Hold the frame in one hand and keep the sticks in place. With the other hand, wrap the yarn over and around one arm of the X, then over and around the next arm, and so on (Picture 2). Pull the yarn tight each time. Every time you wrap an arm, push the yarn down snugly toward the center. Continue working this way until the god's eye is completed (Picture 3).

You can wrap the entire X with the same color yarn, or you can add different colors. To start a new color, tie the end of the old color yarn to an arm of the X. Make a double knot. Now start a new color of yarn in the same place by tying it on. Continue wrapping. You can add as many colors as you like. Once you get the hang of making god's eyes, try making a gigantic one using 2 rulers, or a tiny one using toothpicks!

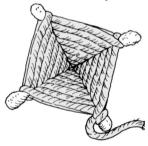

Picture 3

ROLLED PAPER BEADS

Rolled paper beads are colorful and shiny—perfect for making tons of beautiful necklaces and bracelets.

WHAT YOU'LL NEED:

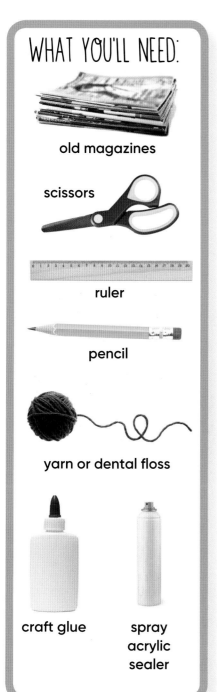

old magazines

scissors

ruler

pencil

yarn or dental floss

craft glue

spray acrylic sealer

Cut out 2 or 3 colorful pages from a magazine. Use a ruler to mark an inch along the long edge of a magazine page. Continue making inch marks along the page. Starting at the first 1-inch mark, cut a long triangle from the magazine page. Repeat until you have 20 to 30 triangles.

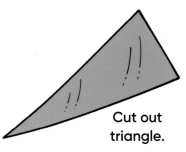

Cut out triangle.

Starting with the wide end of the triangle, roll it around a pencil. Continue rolling until you reach the point of the triangle. Place a dot of glue at the point of the paper, and smooth the point down. Slide the paper bead off the pencil. Repeat until you've made 20 to 30 beads, depending on how long you want your necklace to be.

Roll a triangle onto a pencil.

String the beads on yarn or dental floss. Tie the ends together in a double knot. Spread newspaper over your work surface, and place the necklace on the newspaper. With an adult's help, spray acrylic sealer to give your beads a shiny finish.

String beads on yarn or dental floss.

PASTA LACE ORNAMENTS

These decorations not only make exquisite Christmas tree ornaments—they also look very pretty hanging in a window.

WHAT YOU'LL NEED:

waxed paper

food coloring

small bowls

pasta wheels

elbow macaroni

craft glue

ribbon

Cover your work surface with waxed paper. Mix some water and one color food coloring together in a small bowl. Repeat for other colors. Dip 7 pasta wheels and 6 elbow macaroni pieces in the bowls, alternating colors. Let all pasta pieces dry.

Arrange 6 pasta wheels in a circular pattern with 1 pasta wheel in the center. Apply glue to the sides of the pasta wheels and glue them together. Glue the 6 elbow macaroni pieces around the circle of pasta wheels. To make an ornament hanger, bring the ends of a small piece of ribbon together to form a loop. Glue the ends to the back of the ornament.

A typical Ukrainian Christmas tree usually features a spider-and-web ornament for good luck. Legend has it that, long ago, a poor woman with nothing to put on her children's Christmas tree woke on Christmas morning to find the branches covered with spiderwebs turned to silver by the rising sun.

BUTTONS & BROOCHES

Recycle your favorite magazines or greeting cards by turning them into custom jewelry—it's as easy as cut, paste, and wear.

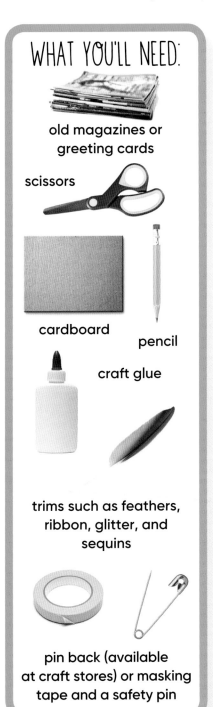

WHAT YOU'LL NEED:

old magazines or greeting cards

scissors

cardboard

pencil

craft glue

trims such as feathers, ribbon, glitter, and sequins

pin back (available at craft stores) or masking tape and a safety pin

Cut a picture from your favorite magazine or greeting card. Place it on a piece of cardboard and trace around it. Cut out the picture shape from the cardboard. This will be your back piece. Glue the picture to the cardboard back piece. Let the glue set. Glue on trims, such as feathers, sequins, ribbon, or glitter, to decorate your brooch. Glue a pin back to the back of the brooch, or tape a safety pin on the back.

BOOK OF PROMISES

Sometimes the best gift doesn't cost a penny. Give a promise worth a million bucks to mom or dad.

WHAT YOU'LL NEED:

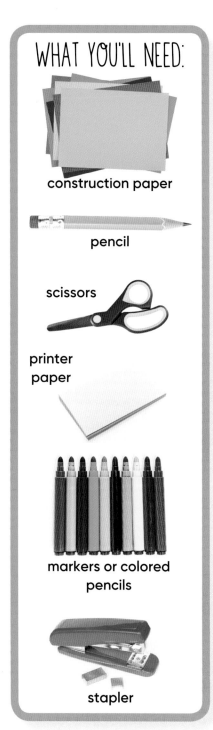

construction paper

pencil

scissors

printer paper

markers or colored pencils

stapler

To make a cover for your book, fold a piece of construction paper in half. Draw a heart as shown, and cut it out. Make sure you don't cut along the fold in the paper at the top of the heart! Fold 3 pieces of printer paper together. Trace the heart on the top piece of paper, and cut it out. Write a promise on each page—they can be serious or silly. Decorate the pages with pictures to illustrate your promise. Insert these pages into the cover, and staple the spine.

I promise to help with the dishes

The practice of bookbinding began in the second century for the protection of old parchment manuscripts. By the Middle Ages the art of bookbinding had risen to great heights. Books were rare and precious, and many were covered with beautiful designs that were true works of art.

YARN COLLAGE

Yarn gives this picture a furry, three-dimensional appearance. Stringing beads on the yarn adds even greater depth.

WHAT YOU'LL NEED:

pencil

drawing or construction paper

craft glue

assorted colors of yarn

scissors

beads (optional)

Draw a picture, such as a plane in the sky, on a piece of drawing or construction paper. Apply a line of glue along the outline of the picture. Then place yarn along the glue. To "color in" a space, spread glue on the inside of the picture and coil the yarn around itself until the space is filled in. Keep outlining and filling all the spaces in your picture with yarn. Trim off any excess yarn. To add more dimension to the picture, you can string a few beads on the yarn as you go along.

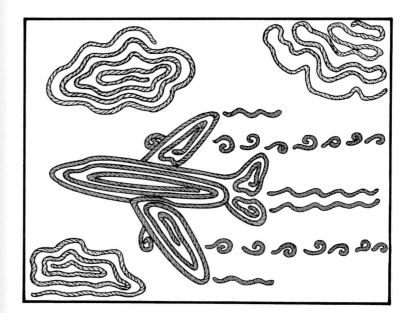

BAG PUPPETS

*Create lots of cute characters and put on a show
for your friends and family.*

WHAT YOU'LL NEED:

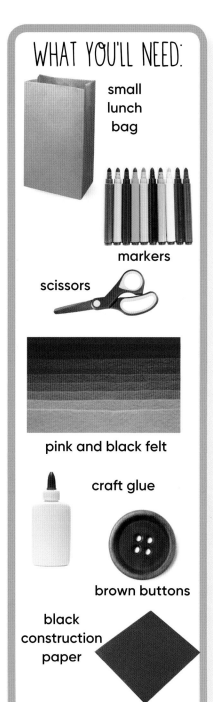

small lunch bag

markers

scissors

pink and black felt

craft glue

brown buttons

black construction paper

You can make all kinds of puppets from bags. To get started, design a hound dog. The bottom of the bag will become the top of the dog's head. Color big spots on the bag. Use the crease of the bag for a mouth. Cut out a pink felt tongue and glue it inside the crease.

Glue 2 brown buttons for eyes. Add some fringed black construction paper for eyelashes. Cut 2 long ears from black felt. Glue an ear to each side of the bag. Put on a show, and have your puppet sing "Hound Dog."

In Thailand, the ancient art of shadow puppetry is enjoying new popularity. The performance is so beautiful that many years ago it was said that one play shook the whole city of Bangkok. Master craftsmen then created a whole set of puppets called "Shaking the City," which were used only for royal functions and special occasions.

HATS: WILD & STYLED

Old birthday or holiday wrapping paper makes great dress-up hats.

WHAT YOU'LL NEED:

wrapping
paper

scissors

craft glue

old
paintbrush

balloon or
large ball

trims such as
feathers, ribbons,
or rhinestones

Make a serious hat for parties, a silly hat just for laughs, or a theme hat for a costume. Cut 2 big identical circles out of wrapping paper. Mix equal parts of water and glue together. Using an old paintbrush, coat the wrong side of one piece of wrapping paper with glue. Place the other piece, wrong side down, over the glue. Place it on your head and form it into a hat shape while the glue is still wet. Once you have shaped the hat, place it over a blown-up balloon or a large ball. Let the hat set overnight. When it is dry, decorate it with feathers, ribbons, glitter, or rhinestones.

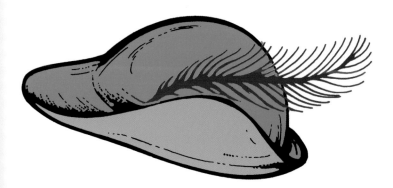

STAINED GLASS HEART

The contrast between a black background and colored tissue paper makes your design pop out.

WHAT YOU'LL NEED:

black construction paper

light-colored pencil or chalk

scissors

colored tissue paper

craft glue

Fold a piece of black construction paper in half. Using a piece of chalk or a light pencil, draw half of a heart shape along the fold. Draw shapes inside the heart to cut out. Cut out the heart shape as well as the inside shapes,

then glue different colors of tissue paper on the back of the paper to cover the inside cut-out shapes. Hang this "stained glass" paper heart in a window so that light shines through it. You can also make stained-glass paper snowflakes using this technique.

Even though the roots of Valentine's Day go back to A.D. 496, the custom of sending specially printed cards to celebrate the holiday did not become common until the 1780s. These cards were an especially big hit in Germany, where they were called "friendship cards."

CHARM BAG

Charm bags hold small objects that bring good luck or happy memories. Make your own, and you'll have a private place for all the cool stuff you find.

WHAT YOU'LL NEED:

1 piece of cloth or felt (4x12 inches)

1 piece of string or cord (at least 10 inches long)

needle and thread (or sewing machine)

Ask an adult for help before you begin.

Fold the short end of the cloth down 1 inch, making a flap (Picture 1). Sew the flap to the cloth about $\frac{1}{4}$ inch from the edge. Leave the ends open (Picture 2). Follow the same steps for the other end of the cloth. This makes 2 "tubes" at opposite ends of the cloth (Picture 3). Later, you will put a piece of string through these tubes to make a drawstring. Next, fold the cloth in half. If the cloth has a pattern, fold so the pattern is on the inside (Picture 4). Sew the sides of the cloth together, about $\frac{1}{4}$ inch in from the edge. Stop sewing right before you reach the tubes (Picture 5). Turn your charm bag inside out. Push a piece of string through both tubes and tie the ends of the string together (Picture 6).

Picture 1

Picture 2

Picture 3

Picture 4

Picture 5

Picture 6

JIGSAW PUZZLE

Nothing to do on a rainy day? Make this jigsaw puzzle for hours of fun.

WHAT YOU'LL NEED:

posterboard

pencil

markers

magazine
(optional)

scissors

craft glue

Sketch a picture on a piece of posterboard and color it in with markers. Or, if you'd rather, cut out a picture from a magazine and glue it on the posterboard. To divide the picture into puzzle pieces, turn the posterboard over and use the pencil to draw separate puzzle sections. The bigger the sections, the easier your puzzle will be. Add knobs to each piece at the spot where the puzzle pieces will interlock. (See illustration.) Cut out the puzzle pieces. Now you can put your puzzle back together again!

What do a map of Europe and a jigsaw puzzle have in common? Back in the 1760s, European mapmakers glued maps onto wood and cut them into small pieces. These early jigsaw puzzles helped children learn geography! American children still find out about places in the world by putting together puzzle maps.

MATCH-UP BOOKS

Create your own collection of kooky characters.

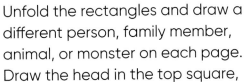

WHAT YOU'LL NEED:

2 sheets of white paper
(8½x11 inches)

pencil or crayons

lightweight
cardboard

scissors

stapler

Cut 2 sheets of paper each into 3 equal-sized rectangles. (Cut across the short side of the paper.) This gives you 6 rectangles. Stack the 6 paper rectangles on top of each other. Fold them down twice, dividing the papers into 3 sections.

Unfold the rectangles and draw a different person, family member, animal, or monster on each page. Draw the head in the top square, the body in the middle square, and the legs in the bottom. (NOTE: The drawings should all be about the same size, and the heads, bodies, and legs should all line up in the same place.

After you finish drawing, cut a piece of lightweight cardboard to the same size as one of the rectangles. Put this piece of cardboard on the bottom of the stack. Then staple the left side of your drawings together and to the cardboard to make a book. Carefully cut across the papers along the folds, stopping before you get to the staples. (Don't cut through the cardboard!) Your book is done. Flip through your book, turning different flaps at a time, to see what silly characters you can create!

SEWING CARDS

Who says you need needle and thread to sew? Use yarn to decorate these special shapes that you cut out.

WHAT YOU'LL NEED:

**sturdy cardboard
(measuring about
6x6 inches for
each card)**

pencil

scissors

hole punch

**yarn
(about 2 feet for
each card)**

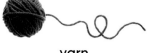

clear tape

Make several outline drawings—animals, people, whatever you want—on several pieces of cardboard, then cut out the shapes. Punch holes around the edges every $\frac{1}{2}$ inch or so. Next, tie a knot in one end of a piece of yarn, then wrap a small piece of tape around the other end (just like on the end of a shoe-lace) so that you can easily push the yarn through the holes in the cardboard. Sew the card by threading the holes with different pieces of colored yarn.

You can even try sewing different pieces together to make 3-dimensional shapes. For example, sew 6 squares together to make a cube. Sew 8 triangles to make a diamond, or 4 triangles and 1 square to make a pyramid. What other shapes can you make?

MINIATURE EASEL

Display different art projects as often as you like with a craft stick easel.

Cover your work surface with newspaper. Decorate 5 craft sticks with acrylic paint. Let the paint dry. Glue 3 sticks in the shape of an A. Glue a fourth stick perpendicular to the crosspiece to make the art stand. To make a hinge, cut a 1-inch square out of cardboard. Fold the square in half. Glue it to the back of the point of the A-frame. Glue the last stick to the other side of the cardboard. Let the glue set, then stand the easel up and put your pictures on display.

In museums such as the Louvre in Paris, home of the *Mona Lisa*, student artists are at work. The students set up their easels and art supplies in the middle of the exhibit areas, quietly recreating their own versions of the most famous paintings in the world.

SPIRAL MOBILE

Hang your mobile in front of an open window and let the wind gently twirl and whirl your spiral.

WHAT YOU'LL NEED:

pencil

39-ounce-size plastic coffee can lid

scissors

acrylic paints and paintbrush

string

hole punch

mobile items such as shells, acorns, or beads

To make the spiral mobile hanger, draw a 1-inch-wide spiral line on a large coffee can lid. (See illustration for reference.) With an adult's help, cut along the spiral line. Decorate the spiral mobile hanger with acrylic paints. Let dry.

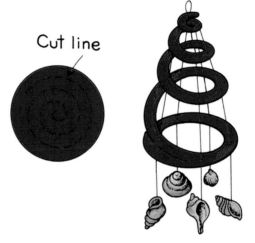

Cut line

Punch holes in the mobile hanger along the spiral, making sure the holes line up together on each ring of the spiral. Punch a hole at the top end of the spiral, and thread it with string to hang the mobile. Pull the spiral hanger open. Tie a piece of string through 1 top hole of the spiral, and string it through 1 hole on each adjacent part of the spiral. Leave the end of the string hanging. This is where you will hang your mobile items. Repeat for remaining holes. Hang shells, acorns, or beads from each string end.

Ask an adult for help before you begin.

BERRY BASKET WEAVING

This great basket will hold your treasures. Fill it with dried flowers or candy treats. It makes a great gift, too.

WHAT YOU'LL NEED:

plastic berry basket

fabric or ribbon

scissors

construction paper

stapler

tissue paper

Cut several strips of fabric or ribbon as wide as the openings in your basket. Weave the strips in and out of the slots around the basket. Tie each strip in a knot and trim the excess. To make a handle, cut a 1-inch-wide strip of construction paper. Secure 1 end of the strip to each side of the basket with a stapler. If you want, use a strip of fabric or ribbon to tie a bow around the handle. Line your basket with tissue paper, then fill it with goodies.

Hopi Indian weavers are carrying on one of the oldest art traditions in the world. Woven in brilliant colors, as well as black and white, Hopi weavings are symbols for what is most important in Hopi life. In the women's basket dance, for example, woven plaques are made to honor the earth.

YEAR-ROUND WREATH

Who says wreaths are only for Christmas? Challenge yourself to design a wreath for each month of the year.

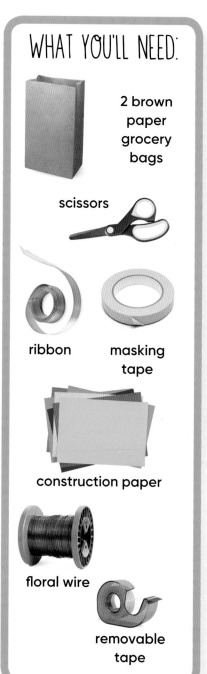
Cut off the bottom of a grocery bag, and cut a seam down one side to make a large sheet. Repeat with the other bag.

Cut a grocery bag.

Place the bags on top of each other. Roll the bags together to make one long log. Twist the roll and then form it into a circle. Tape the two ends together. This is the wreath base. Tie a piece of ribbon into a bow, and use a piece of floral wire to attach it to the wreath. Decorate the wreath with paper cutouts for each month. From construction paper, cut out January snowflakes, February hearts, March shamrocks, and so on. Attach the cutouts to the wreath using removable tape. Change the cutouts and the ribbon each month.

Tape ends together, forming a circle.

"WHEN I WAS YOUNG" BOOK

Celebrate your ancestry and learn about history with a book about your grandparents.

WHAT YOU'LL NEED:

construction paper

stapler

markers

old magazines

scissors

craft glue

Your grandparents have led a long and full life. They probably have had experiences that seem unbelievable to you. They didn't have computer games! What did your grandparents do for fun when they were your age? Did they go to school? What was it like? What kinds of food did they eat? What clothes did they wear? Who were their friends? What did they dream they would be when they grew up?

Get to know your grandparents. Ask them to tell you stories about their lives when they were your age, and make sure you take notes or record the conversation. Then staple folded sheets of construction paper together to make a book. Write a story inside about some of the things your grandparents told you. Draw pictures or cut out photos from old magazines to illustrate their story.

Use markers to write a title, such as "The Story of Grandpa and Grandma," on the cover of your book. This is one book the whole family will cherish forever!

What was your favorite toy?

A train

SAILBOATS

Sailboat racing is a time-honored sport. Make your own bathtub competition with these tiny floating boats.

WHAT YOU'LL NEED:

ballpoint pen

clean foam meat trays

scissors

permanent markers

straight pin

glue

Use a ballpoint pen to draw a boat hull and a triangular sail on foam trays. Cut the pieces out. Decorate them with permanent markers. Draw a sail emblem and your boat's name. Put a line of glue (it's waterproof) on the boat hull and stand up the sail in the glue. Use a straight pin to keep the sail straight until the glue dries. Make a fleet and have bathtub races. You can blow your boats from the start to the finish line!

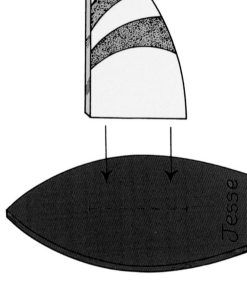

The America's Cup is the most sought-after trophy in sailboat racing even though there is no prize money awarded to the winner. First awarded in the mid-19th century, the trophy was originally named "The 100 Guinea Cup," which was what it was worth in British currency at that time.

CROSSWORD PUZZLE

This crossword puzzle has a surprising twist because the clues are pictures instead of words.

WHAT YOU'LL NEED:

graph paper

pencil

tracing paper

markers

black felt-tip pen

Think of words to go in your crossword puzzle, making sure one word can connect with another word. Make your answer key using a piece of graph paper. Draw a square for each letter of each word in your puzzle, connecting the words with a shared letter. Write each letter in. Then number each word going across and each word going down. This is the answer key.

Cover the crossword puzzle with tracing paper to copy the squares without the letters in them, or redraw the puzzle without the letters on a new sheet of graph paper. On a new piece of paper, draw a clue for each word, and number the clues to match the words. If the word for 1 across is dog, then draw a dog for clue 1 across. Draw a decorative border around the puzzle. Make photocopies of the cross-word puzzle to give to your friends and family.

ARTIST!

You'll need to be quick on the draw to do well in this game.

WHAT YOU'LL NEED:

paper

pencil

cup or hat

watch

Before you begin, ask someone who won't be playing with you to write down some famous sayings or parts of songs. Have the person write each one on a small, separate piece of paper and then fold it. Put these pieces of paper into a cup or hat. If younger kids are playing, you can write down names of animals or objects that they can draw instead of songs or sayings.

The first player chooses a piece of paper from the cup. Then he or she draws clues on paper so the other players can guess what the phrase is. Of course, you can't use letters or numbers—that would be spelling, not drawing!

You'd better be quick on the draw; you only have 2 minutes to get your point across. If someone guesses your word or phrase in that time, you get 1 point. If not, you get no points. Either way, it's someone else's turn to be the Artist.

RUBBER BAND ZITHER

Bet you didn't think you could make music from a box! Play high and low notes with this homemade instrument.

WHAT YOU'LL NEED:

shoe box with lid

markers

scissors

corrugated cardboard

craft glue

rubber bands

Decorate the shoe box with markers. With an adult's help, cut a 4-inch-square hole in the lid. Cut two 1x4½-inch pieces from a piece of corrugated cardboard. Cut a zigzag edge on each piece, creating cardboard "combs." Glue one "comb" to one side of the square hole, and glue the other "comb" slightly angled from the square on the other side. Let the glue set overnight. Stretch rubber bands from the teeth of one comb to the teeth of the other comb on the shoe box lid. Put the lid on the box. Pluck the rubber bands to play your zither.

Essentially, a zither is a wooden sound box dating back to at least the year 2000 B.C. Unlike a guitar or violin (other instruments that are plucked), the zither has no "neck."

PERSONAL PLACE MATS

It doesn't even matter if you get these place mats dirty, because they wipe clean with a damp sponge. Now that's neat!

WHAT YOU'LL NEED:

markers

12x18-inch piece of posterboard

scissors

cutouts from construction paper or old magazines

craft glue

Use markers to draw a background, such as a beach, on a piece of the posterboard. Cut out shapes or pictures from construction paper or old magazines. If your background is a beach scene, cut out boats and people. Glue the cutouts on the posterboard. Ask an adult to take you to a copy center store to have your place mat laminated. Leave a $\frac{1}{4}$-inch plastic border around the place mat.

You can also make place mats out of fun things you want to study, such as maps, sports facts, or poems. Another idea is to draw a maze on your place mat. Once it's laminated, use a grease pencil and play the game again and again.

A-MAZE-ING

Create your own maze game to play with your friends.

WHAT YOU'LL NEED:

pencil

tracing paper

black
felt-tip pen

colored pencils

Use a pencil to draw a zigzag track on tracing paper. Add detours and dead ends off the track, and add more tracks that go nowhere. You can also make more maze tracks that are curved or triangular. Once you've completed the maze, go over it with a black felt-tip pen. Add a drawing at the entrance and exit, such as a lost bear (entrance) looking for its den (exit). Color the maze with colored pencils. Make copies of your maze game and give it to your friends to play.

SCRAPBOOK BINDING

Save memories from a vacation, jot down your thoughts, or sketch drawings in your own special book.

WHAT YOU'LL NEED:

two 11x2-inch pieces of cardboard (for the panels)

two 11x12-inch pieces of cardboard (for the covers)

two 17x20-inch pieces of cloth

scissors

List continued on next page

Using the illustration as your guide, place 1 cardboard panel piece and 1 cardboard cover piece on 1 piece of cloth. Leave a $\frac{1}{4}$-inch space between the cardboard pieces. Cut out the corners from the cloth.

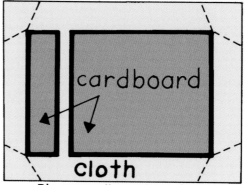

Place cardboard on cloth.

Remove the cover board from its position, and, using an old paintbrush, apply an even coat of glue on one side of the board. Place it back onto the back of the cloth to glue it in place. Repeat with the panel board. Fold the cloth over the boards and glue in place. Let the glue set.

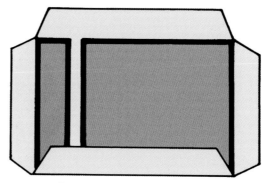

Fold cloth over cardboard.

SCRAPBOOK BINDING

Cut a 7x7-inch square from a piece of paper. Glue the square of paper over the cloth edges on the cover board.

old paintbrush

craft glue

printer or construction paper

hole punch

yarn

Glue a square of paper over cloth edges.

Repeat these steps to make the other cover.

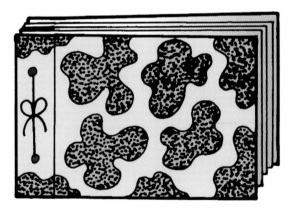

Tie pieces together.

Punch 2 holes in the panels of the front and back covers, making sure the holes line up together. To make the inside pages, punch 2 holes in several sheets of printer or construction paper in the same position as the cover holes. Tie the scrapbook together using yarn.

WAITING KIT

No more boring waiting rooms with nothing interesting to do. This project creates activities for you to do anytime, anywhere.

WHAT YOU'LL NEED:

10x24-inch piece of muslin

needle and thread

yarn or string

cardboard

fabric paint or permanent markers

Hem the 2 short ends of the muslin. Fold the muslin in half, bringing the 2 hemmed ends together, with the hems facing out. Cut a few small holes in the hemmed ends for the drawstring. Thread a piece of yarn or string through the holes and tie it in a knot. Sew the 2 side seams closed. Turn the bag inside out.

Place a piece of cardboard inside the bag. Decorate the bag with permanent markers or fabric paint. When the paint is dry, remove the cardboard.

Fill the bag with a notepad, colored pencils, crayons, scissors, a glue stick, a travel game, and a good book.

Should you watch out for falling heels and soles? Not really. But if you're waiting anxiously for something to be finished, people might say you're "waiting for the other shoe to drop."

CHAPTER 3
SCIENCE AND NATURE PROJECTS

MOON ROCK RELAY

Step quickly on these moon rocks to race to the moon and back.

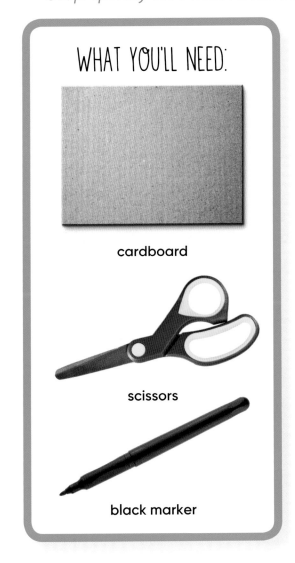

WHAT YOU'LL NEED:

cardboard

scissors

black marker

Play this game to see which team of astronauts can blast off to the moon and back first. Cut 6 large rock shapes out of cardboard and use a black marker to color them so they look like moon rocks. Divide players into two teams. Mark the start of the racecourse with a cardboard sign that says Earth. Place a sign that says Moon about 20 feet away.

To play, the first player on each team has to toss out 3 moon rocks and step on them, each time picking up the back rock and moving it forward toward the moon. The players can only move forward by stepping on the moon rocks. When the player reaches the moon, she or he picks up the moon rocks, tosses them out again, and repeats the process to get back to Earth as quickly as possible. When the first player gets safely back to Earth, it's time for the next player on the team to go to the moon and back. The first team to send all its astronauts to the moon and back is the winner.

SPECKLED PLANTS

Make a mosaic to show the many colors of plants.

WHAT YOU'LL NEED:

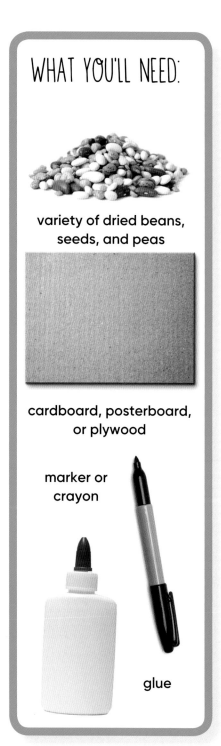

variety of dried beans, seeds, and peas

cardboard, posterboard, or plywood

marker or crayon

glue

Start with a trip to a grocery store. (If possible, go to one that sells a wide variety of beans and peas in bulk, so you can buy just a handful of each.) Check out all the different kinds of dried (not canned) beans and peas. You should find beans in black, red, brown, white, and speckles. You'll find bright green peas and light green lima beans. Lentils come in many colors, including pink! Don't forget to check out seeds, too: tiny black poppy seeds, striped sunflower seeds, green pumpkin seeds, and whatever else strikes your fancy.

Collect as many different shapes, sizes, and colors of beans and seeds as you can. Then use them to make a mosaic. Make a drawing on a piece of cardboard, posterboard, or plywood. Then glue on beans and seeds to fill in your drawing.

PRESTO CHANGE-O!

Seawater contains salt, which makes it unfit to drink. Here's how can you change saltwater to freshwater.

WHAT YOU'LL NEED:

pot

water

salt

aluminum foil

bowl

Fill a pot with water. Now put in some salt. This is your "seawater." Use aluminum foil to make a "tent" that covers the pot and slopes over a wide, shallow bowl. With adult help, bring the water to a boil.

As the water boils and turns to steam, the steam will condense on the foil and drip into the bowl. Let most of the water move from the pot to the bowl. Then let the water cool.

Look at the water in the bowl and taste it. How is it different from the water in the pot? What happened to the salt? This method of making freshwater is called "distillation," and it is used to help provide drinking water to areas where only seawater is available.

Ask an adult for help before you begin!

SPORE PRINTS

Did you know that mushooms can make their own prints?

WHAT YOU'LL NEED:

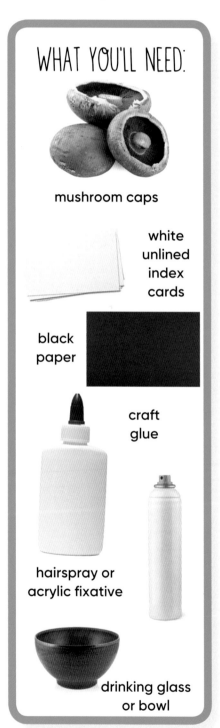

mushroom caps

white unlined index cards

black paper

craft glue

hairspray or acrylic fixative

drinking glass or bowl

Find a mushroom in the wild, or get some from the store. (Be careful when handling wild mushrooms—don't eat them because some wild mushrooms are poisonous!) Make sure you find some with the caps open. Look underneath the cap. The gills inside are lined with structures that make and release spores by the millions. Each spore can grow into a new fungus.

Cover half of an index card with black paper. Pop out the stem from the mushroom cap and place the cap on the card so that half is on the black paper and half on the white. Cover with a glass or bowl and let the cap sit overnight. The next day remove the glass and the mushroom cap. You should see a print of the mushroom spores. Pale spores will show up on the black paper, while darker ones will show on the white. Ask an adult to spray the print with hairspray or acrylic fixative to keep it from smearing.

MAGNETIC MINERALS

Is there iron in your cereal? With a little help from science, you can perform some breakfast table magic.

The iron your body requires in order to make healthy blood is the same iron that is found in the earth. If the cereal you eat for breakfast is high in iron, it should be attracted to a magnet.

Put some cereal in a plastic bag and use a rolling pin to crush it into powder. Then, touch the magnet to the powder. Does the cereal cling to the magnet? If so, you're well on your way to fulfilling your daily iron requirement!

WHAT YOU'LL NEED:

cereal

plastic bag

rolling pin

strong magnet

Many years ago, sailors used chunks of lodestone (a form of the mineral iron that acts as a natural magnet) to make compasses. Some ancient sailors even believed in Magnetic Mountain, a huge lodestone to which all compasses pointed. It was said that if you sailed too close, Magnetic Mountain would pull every nail out of your ship!

THE LIVING OCEAN

Oceans don't just contain saltwater. They encompass many different living things. Make a diorama of this underwater world.

WHAT YOU'LL NEED:

book about the ocean

shoe box

markers or paint

paper

scissors

decorations

When you think of the ocean, you probably think about swimming at the beach or going for a boat ride. Those are fun things, but they're not the only ways oceans are used. Oceans are home to many unusual and delicate forms of life, such as starfish, algae, seahorses, coral, anemones, and a variety of fish.

Find a book about sea life, and learn about all the different things that are found in the world's oceans. Then choose a part of the ocean and make a diorama that shows what you learned. You may want to show a coral reef, or a deep part of the ocean. What kind of animals or plants live there? On the inside bottom of a shoe box, draw or paint a blue background to represent water. You can cut and color paper fish and plants and glue them to the background. Then turn the shoe box on its side and make the "floor" of your ocean. You might put in sand and shells, or make plants and animals (such as lobsters or crabs) out of clay to populate your ocean. You can also hang paper fish from strings taped to the "ceiling" of the box.

TWISTER IN A BOTTLE

Most real tornadoes are made of air, but you can demonstrate how tornadoes work using water.

WHAT YOU'LL NEED:

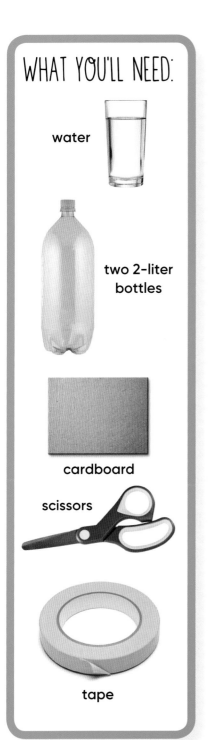

water

two 2-liter bottles

cardboard

scissors

tape

Pour water into a 2-liter plastic bottle until it is about $\frac{3}{4}$ full. Cut a circle of cardboard as big around as the bottle's opening. Then cut a $\frac{1}{4}$-inch hole in the center. Place the cardboard circle on top of your water bottle's opening. Turn another 2-liter bottle upside down and tape the two bottles together, top to top.

Wrap the bottle necks with tape so the connection doesn't leak. Now hold the bottles so the full bottle is upside-down on top. With one hand, hold the bottom bottle to steady it. With the other hand, begin moving the top bottle in a circle. Watch what happens: a tornado in a bottle.

Water tornadoes, such as the one you just made, happen in nature, too. When a tornado forms over water, it's called a waterspout.

TERRIFIC TURTLES

Turtles have been around since the days when dinosaurs walked the earth—millions of years ago. Here's how to make your own turtle "pet rock."

WHAT YOU'LL NEED:

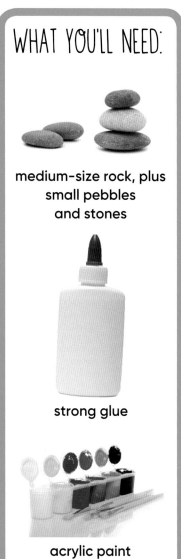

medium-size rock, plus small pebbles and stones

strong glue

acrylic paint and paintbrush

To create your turtle, begin with a medium-size rock. This will be your turtle's body and shell. Then, find four pebbles to use for the feet. These pebbles should all be about the same size. Glue the pebbles onto the rock using strong glue, leaving room at one end for the head. Now find a stone slightly larger than the feet to be your turtle's head, and glue it in place. Let the glue dry.

Once the glue dries, it is time to decorate your pet turtle. Paint a face, and then paint a colorful design on its shell. (You can look in a reference book to see some examples, or you can come up with your own design.)

Do you know the difference between a turtle and a tortoise? A turtle refers to all shelled reptiles, but a tortoise is a type of turtle that lives entirely on the land. Turtles come in all sizes. Some can grow as big as 1,200 pounds and live as long as 100 years.

CLOUDS OVERHEAD

A good way to remember the different clouds is to make a mobile.

WHAT YOU'LL NEED:

posterboard

scissors

cotton balls

glue

string

dowel rod

acrylic paint
and paintbrush

For each kind of cloud, cut its shape out of poster-board. Glue cotton balls to both sides of the shape to make it look like a cloud. Make each cloud look like the real thing as much as you can. For a cumulus cloud, bunch up lots of cotton balls to make it fluffy. For a cirrus cloud, stretch out the cotton balls to make them thin and wispy. Nimbostratus clouds are gray, multilevel, and often dark. You could use a little gray paint (just mix a little black into white) to make some of the clouds gray.

When all your clouds are assembled and the glue is dry, make a small hole in the top of each one. Then tie a piece of string through each hole. Nimbostratus clouds should have the longest string, since they're closest to Earth. Cirrus clouds should have the shortest string, since they're the highest clouds.

Now tie each piece of string to a dowel rod. Finally, tie a piece of string around the middle of the dowel, and use it to hang your mobile.

SWEET CRYSTALS

In this activity, you'll do two things at once: see how crystals form in nature and make candy!

WHAT YOU'LL NEED:

water

sugar

saucepan

spoon

glass jar

string

pencil

craft stick

With the help of an adult, boil ½ cup water in a saucepan. Add a cup of sugar one spoonful at a time until all the sugar is dissolved. Keep adding sugar until the solution turns into a clear syrup. Let it cool for about 10 minutes, then pour the syrup into a glass jar.

Now get a piece of string about 6 inches long. Tie one end of the string around a pencil, then tie the other end to a craft stick. Put the pencil on top of the jar so the craft stick hangs in the syrup.

Set your "crystal maker" aside. Take a look at it every day to see what's happening. In about a week, the syrup should be crystallized and ready to eat.

Ask an adult for help before you begin!

MR. AND MRS. SPRING

These green pepper people are bursting with springtime color and fun!

WHAT YOU'LL NEED:

green peppers

kitchen knife

toothpicks

assorted cut-up vegetables such as broccoli, celery, and green olives

bunch of fresh parsley

Wash and dry 2 green peppers. With an adult's help, cut off the very top and scoop out the insides. Cut 4 triangles from the discarded tops of the peppers. Stick triangle-shaped pieces of green pepper on the ends of toothpicks and poke them into the pepper bodies to make arms. Two-inch pieces of celery stuck on the ends of toothpicks can be attached to the bottom of the peppers to make legs or feet. Attach other vegetable pieces in this way to make the face: green olive slices for eyes, a broccoli-flower nose, and a half-circle of red pepper for the mouth. Fill the top of the peppers with a sprig of fresh parsley to make hair. Be as creative as you can be in making interesting or original faces. Then invite Mr. and Mrs. Spring to lunch!

Ask an adult for help before you begin!

FALLING STARS

For ages untold, humans looked up at the summer night sky and shuddered in fear or sighed in amazement as the stars seemed to fall from the sky!

WHAT YOU'LL NEED:

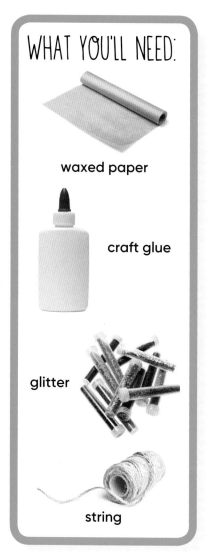

waxed paper

craft glue

glitter

string

You don't have to wait until dark to fill your room with falling stars! Use glue to outline as many 5-pointed stars as you want on a sheet of waxed paper. Be sure to include 3 lines for a "tail" so the stars look like they are falling. All of your glue lines should be wide and thick. Sprinkle the glue with glitter until the lines are completely covered, then let your stars sit until the glue is completely dry. (This may take as long as two days.) When the glue is no longer tacky to the touch, peel the stars off the waxed paper and use string to hang your falling stars from the ceiling. In the dark, you can shine a flashlight on the stars to make them sparkle and glow.

A CREEPY CRAWLY GAME

Here's a fun game you can play with your friends.
The object is to be the first to make your own "beetle."

This is a game for two or more players. Each player needs a sheet of drawing paper and some markers. You will roll the dice to draw a beetle. Here's what you must roll to draw each part:

1	head	7	leg
2	body	8	leg
3	leg	9	eye
4	leg	10	eye
5	leg	11	antenna
6	leg	12	antenna

Roll both dice each time, but only draw one beetle part for each roll. Here are two examples to show you how it works:

Let's say you roll a 1 and a 2. You can draw either the beetle's head (1) or body (2), but not both. Or, you can draw a leg, because 1 plus 2 equals 3, and a 3 lets you draw a leg.

If your beetle already has the parts for which you rolled, your turn is over.

Use different colors to make your beetle special. Whoever finishes his or her beetle first wins.

FOGGY NOTIONS

Did you ever wonder what exactly fog is? This project will help clear up the mystery.

WHAT YOU'LL NEED:

bottle

hot water

rubbing alcohol

ice cubes

Ask an adult for help before you begin!

You've probably seen fog. That's because when fog is around, it's about all you can see. Well, fog is a cloud that forms very close to the ground. In nature, when a mass of cold air bumps into a mass of warm humid air, millions of tiny droplets of water are formed. That's fog. Here's a way to get some cold air and some warm air together and make fog:

Fill a bottle $\frac{1}{3}$ full with very hot water. Ask an adult to add a few drops of rubbing alcohol. Put a piece of ice over the top of the bottle, and watch fog develop.

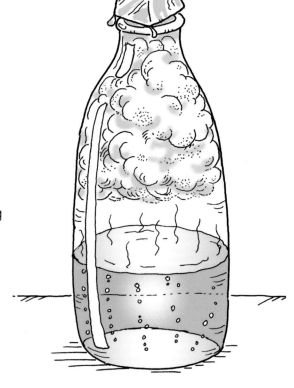

INVENT A FLOWER

There are lots of interesting flowers in nature. Try to create your own.

WHAT YOU'LL NEED:

parts of flowers and plants cut out from photographs

scissors

craft glue

posterboard or cardboard

Can you guess just how big the world's biggest flowers are? Well, they're called rafflesia, and they can be as big as 3 feet wide and weigh as much as 15 pounds. They have almost no leaves and no stems—they're all flower! You've probably never seen one, since they only grow in the rain forests of Indonesia. Other unusual flowers include the bee flower, which looks so much like a bee that real bees get confused. And there's actually a flower called the carrion flower ("carrion" means dead flesh) that looks and smells like dead meat.

What wild kinds of flowers can you come up with? Find out by inventing a flower. Cut out plant and flower parts (leaves, stems, flowers, seeds, etc.) from pictures in old magazines. Glue the parts together on a piece of cardboard or posterboard to make a crazy new flower.

Have you ever wondered why flowers have so many colors? Nature gives flowers bright colors to attract birds and insects. As the birds and insects fly, they deposit pollen from one flower into another. This allows the flowers to start making seeds.

WHAT'S YOUR GAME?

It's fun to create your very own nature board game and play it with your friends.

WHAT YOU'LL NEED:

posterboard

index cards

markers

small stones or coins

dice

It may seem hard at first to make up a board game about nature. To get started, choose a theme, such as "save the forest," "clean up that oil spill," or "recycle for life."

Then think of a board game that you like to play. You can use this game as a model for yours. Draw squares throughout your game board as shown, and think of things to write or draw in the squares. Remember, everything in the game should be about nature. For example, you could have a player lose a turn for throwing trash in a river, or move ahead for picking up trash. Use your imagination!

Be sure to write down rules for your game. Again, use the rules from one of your games as a guide. Finally, try playing your game, using small stones or coins as playing pieces. You may find there are things you need to change. Keep working on it until your game goes smoothly!

TIME FLIES

Learn about the parts of the moon's cycle with a lunar phases flipbook.

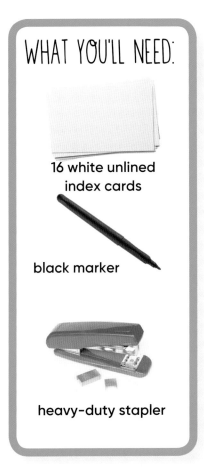
The moon provides a great example of nature's cycles. Every 29½ days, the moon goes through a complete cycle. The moon begins the cycle being invisible to people on Earth. This happens when the moon comes between the sun and Earth, so that sunlight only shines on the backside of the moon, where we can't see it. As the moon moves around Earth, we see more of the sunlit part. Halfway through the cycle we see a full moon. At that time, the whole face of the moon is illuminated by the sun. Then we see less and less of the moon until, finally, it is invisible again.

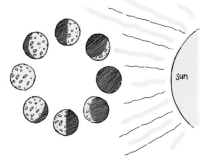

On 16 index cards, draw the phases as shown on this page. Draw each "moon" on the right half of the card. Stack the cards in order, with the first one on top of the stack. Staple all the cards together on the left side, or just hold the cards together firmly. With your right hand, flip through the stack to see the moon's phases.

The moon's surface is covered with thousands of bowl-shaped craters. These craters were formed when rocky meteorites or asteroids crashed into the moon. While most craters are only a few feet wide, the largest ones stretch for more than 50 miles!

'TITES OR 'MITES?

If you sat in a cave for thousands of years, you could watch stalactites and stalagmites form. Or you could make your own in days.

WHAT YOU'LL NEED:

two jars

water

Epsom salts

string

small weights

plate

Fill two jars with warm water. Mix in Epsom salts until no more will dissolve. Wet a piece of string and tie a weight to each end. Drop one end of the string into each jar. Put a plate between the two jars, with the string hanging over the plate.

Check your "cave" at least once a day to see if stalactites and stalagmites have formed. By the way, if you're wondering which are 'tites and which are 'mites: Stalactites have to hold on tight to stay on the ceiling of the cave. Stalagmites have to be mighty to stand up on the floor of the cave.

SEASONAL SILHOUETTES

Think about each season's different colors and various holidays, then use the shades of each season to make a collage.

WHAT YOU'LL NEED:

colored tissue paper

craft glue

brown and black construction paper

white colored pencil

scissors

Glue pieces of colored tissue paper—reds, oranges, and yellows for fall—all over a sheet of brown construction paper. Using a white colored pencil, draw a fall shape on a piece of black construction paper. You might draw a tree, a pumpkin, a cornucopia, or a ghost. Cut the shape out. Glue the silhouette over the tissue paper. Make a frame out of black construction paper, and glue it over the picture. Make other sheets with winter, spring, and summer colors, and use black silhouettes to make seasonal scenes on tissue paper.

Silhouette drawings were very popular in late-18th-century Europe and later in England and America. But what invention made silhouette drawings less popular? You guessed it—the photograph!

WARM, FUZZY SNOW

Use cotton balls to create a 3-D winter scene that won't melt away in the spring.

WHAT YOU'LL NEED:

paint and paintbrush

shoe box

cotton balls

crayons   **glue**

glitter (optional)

Paint the inside of a shoe box. Use a good sky-colored paint such as blue or gray. When the paint is dry, tilt the shoe box on its side. Then make a snow scene using cotton balls as snow. Use your imagination to make snow-covered hills and trees, snow people, snow animals, and more. (If you want to, you can make your drawing in crayon first, then glue on the cotton.) Add glitter to make your snow sparkle like the real thing!

WHERE'S THE NORTH POLE?

What direction are you facing right now? You'll know the answer when you make this handy homemade compass.

WHAT YOU'LL NEED:

pie pan

water

dishwashing liquid

bar magnet

needle

¼-inch slice of cork

Fill a pie pan with water. Add a small amount of dishwashing liquid. Now you'll need to magnetize a needle. To do this, use a bar magnet with the north end marked. Scrape the needle across the north end of the magnet, from the eye of the needle to its point. Do this about 15 times. It's important to scrape the needle in the same direction every time—don't rub it back and forth on the magnet.

Carefully poke the needle through a small piece of cork. Float the cork in the middle of the pie pan. Like magic, the needle will always point north. If you walked far enough in that direction, you'd find yourself at the North Pole! That's because Earth is like a giant magnet, with one end in the North Pole and the other end in the South Pole.

PINECONE CREATURES

What kind of wild, imaginary animals can you make out of pinecones?

WHAT YOU'LL NEED:

pinecones

decorations

chenille stems

craft glue

For each creature, you'll need one large pinecone. You'll also need an assortment of decorations (buttons, beads, scrap cloth, chenille stems, leaves, real or plastic flowers). Use these decorations to turn the pinecone into an imaginary animal. Chenille stems work well for creating legs. When you're done, give your creature a name, and make up a story about it.

Most broad-leaved trees change colors to a brilliant orange, red, or yellow in the fall, but pine trees have needles, not leaves. The needles remain green all year, which makes pine trees perfect for Christmas!

PUFFY FISH

Toilet tissue or newspaper help these fish puff up in 3-D!

colored tissue
paper

pencil

scissors

craft
glue

toilet tissue

Lay two pieces of tissue paper together (one on top of the other). Draw the outline of a fish, then carefully cut the shape out of both pieces of tissue. This will be the front and back of your fish. Decorate it any way you like. You can make it look like a real fish or a funny cartoon one. Next, apply a thin line of glue along the inside edge of the front half of your fish, leaving the tail unglued. Put the two pieces of tissue together and let the glue dry. When it's dry, stuff your fish with toilet tissue to make it puff out! Glue the tail shut.

LET IT RAIN

Drip, drip, drop! Use raindrops to create beautiful and unique paintings you can frame and hang on a wall.

WHAT YOU'LL NEED:

water-soluble paint and paintbrush

markers

posterboard

Use water-soluble paint or markers to make solid blocks of color on posterboard. Then put the paper in the rain for a short time. Watch as the rain "paints" your paper. Take the paper out of the rain when you think the painting is finished (before all the color is washed away). Experiment by making raindrop paintings in a light rain or drizzle, a steady rain, and a real downpour.

Rain forms when growing cloud droplets become too heavy to remain in the cloud and, as a result, fall toward the earth's surface in the form of rain. But did you know that rain can also begin as ice crystals that collect to form large snowflakes? As the falling snow passes into warmer air, the flakes melt and collapse into raindrops.

DRIED FRUIT TREATS

Turn this summer's harvest into tasty winter treats.

WHAT YOU'LL NEED:

assorted fresh fruit

peeler

knife

cookie sheets

nuts

nut grinder

lemon juice

coconut

plastic wrap

Begin with some fresh, ripe fruit without bruises. With adult supervision, peel and slice larger fruits, removing seeds or pits. Slices should be about $\frac{1}{4}$-inch thick. Small berries can be dried whole, but bigger berries (such as strawberries) should be sliced.

To dry fruit: Spread the slices in a single layer on a cookie sheet. Put in an oven set to 150°F and dry until most of the moisture is gone but the fruit is still soft. Since you aren't using preservatives, the fruit will be brown. Pack the pieces into a jar and let them sit a week or so before using. Eat your fruit as it is, or make fruit treats.

To make fruit treats: Measure out about two cups of dried fruit and one cup of nuts. Use a nut grinder to chop up the nuts and fruits finely. Moisten with about a tablespoon of lemon juice. Shape into small balls or logs. Roll in shredded coconut. Wrap each treat in plastic wrap.

Ask an adult for help before you begin!

DAY & NIGHT FLIP STONES

Play a toss game with these painted stones.

WHAT YOU'LL NEED:

smooth, round stone

acrylic paint and paintbrush

clear varnish or nail polish

Cover your work surface with old newspapers. On one side of a smooth, round stone, paint a bright sky-blue background. Make sure you don't get any paint on the other side of the rock. When the blue paint dries, paint a large, smiling sun in the middle of it. When that dries, paint the other side of the stone black. Add a crescent moon when the black background is dry. Paint over both sides of the stone with two or three coats of clear varnish or nail polish to protect the paint. Wait for each coat to dry before adding another.

Now you are ready to play a game of "heads or tails." Take turns calling "day" or "night" and tossing the stone in the air to see if the side you called lands face-up. Keep score and see how many "days" and "nights" you can guess.

FOUR SEASONS TREE

Don't wait for the next holiday—celebrate now with a tree for all seasons.

WHAT YOU'LL NEED:

thin tree branches or twigs

construction paper

scissors

markers or colored pencils

lightweight string or clear tape

vase

Find 4 similar-size branches with several twigs coming off of them. Decorate each branch so it represents either winter, spring, summer, or fall. Cut snowflakes, flowers, bugs, and leaves from construction paper. Decorate the shapes with markers or colored pencils. Tie or tape the shapes on each branch for each of the four seasons. Arrange the branches in a pretty vase to make a colorful centerpiece for a table.

Did you know that without the tilt of the earth's axis we wouldn't have seasons? Instead, the areas around the center of the earth would receive the most sun. It would be about the same temperature all year long.

DREAM WEAVER

Create unique wall hangings from natural materials.

WHAT YOU'LL NEED:

sturdy cardboard

scissors

string

wild plant material for weaving (dried grass, strips of bark peeled from twigs, etc.)

craft glue

First you'll need to create a loom. Take a piece of cardboard just a little larger than the size of the weaving you want to make. Cut a row of slits in the top and bottom ends, making each slit $\frac{1}{4}$ to $\frac{1}{2}$ inch apart (see illustration). Tie a knot in a piece of string, slip the knot into one of the slits to anchor it, then run the string to the slit on the opposite side. Slip the string behind the cardboard to the next slit on the same side, bring it through, then run it across the board again. Keep going until the whole piece of cardboard is strung, like strings on a guitar.

Now collect any kind of natural materials that are long and narrow, such as tall dried grass, strips of dried corn husk or cattail leaves, bark peeled from fallen twigs, or long pine needles. Weave these materials in and out of the strings in any way that pleases you. When your weaving is done, slip the ends of the string off the cardboard. Turn your weaving over, and glue the edges to keep the weaving together.

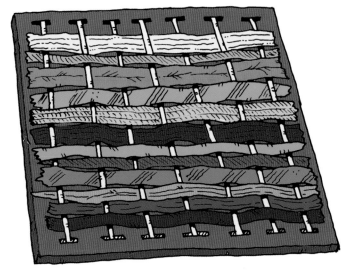

CATERPILLAR PALS

Butterflies and moths are very important pollinators—they carry pollen from flower to flower. And every butterfly or moth starts life as a caterpillar!

WHAT YOU'LL NEED:

light-colored pantyhose or knee-length stockings

scissors

cotton or polyester fiber stuffing

3 small rubber bands

fabric paint

paintbrush

To make a caterpillar pal, tie a knot in the end of a pair of pantyhose. Pull the knot tight. Measure back about 6 inches from the knot, and cut off the rest of the fabric. Turn the tube inside out and stuff it with polyester fiber-fill or cotton. Tie a knot in the other end of the tube to keep the fill in. This knot will be

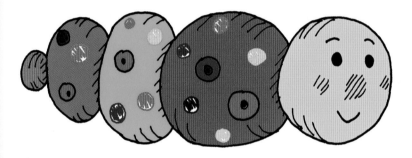

the caterpillar's tail. Trim off any excess material that hangs out of the knot. Wiggle the filler material around until the tube is shaped like a worm. Wrap a rubber band around the caterpillar's body $\frac{1}{3}$ of the way from the nose to the tail. This will create the caterpillar's head. Wrap the second rubber band halfway between the first one and the tail, and the third one halfway between the second rubber band and the tail. Tip: The tighter you wrap the rubber bands, the fatter the caterpillar's parts will be.

Decorate the caterpillar with fabric paint. Let dry.

WHEN IT RAINS, IT POURS

Who says you can't make it rain indoors? No need to wait for a rainy day—just make some rain yourself!

WHAT YOU'LL NEED:

water

saucepan

glass jar with lid

towel

ice cubes

Ask an adult to bring a pot of water to a boil; let it cool slightly. Pour the water into a jar and put on the lid. Place the jar on a towel. Then put ice on the jar's lid. Watch a rainstorm begin in the jar as hot water condenses on the lid and rains down into the water.

Watching your "rainstorm" makes it easy to imagine what happens when a cold front (a mass of cold air) comes into contact with warm air: Moisture from the warm air is pushed up, clouds are formed, and soon it's raining.

It seems to pour almost all the time in some parts of the world! Average annual rainfall varies from less than 1 inch in a desert to over 400 inches in some rain forests.

Ask an adult for help before you begin!

TRAVEL TO OUTER SPACE

Imagine what it would be like to float among the planets, stars, and comets!

WHAT YOU'LL NEED:

scissors

cardboard or heavy paper

markers

decorations (paint, aluminum foil, or glitter)

thread or nylon line

pin

two dowel rods or sticks

If you hang a space mobile in your room, you can look up and imagine you're up there.

Cut out and color shapes to make planets, stars, spaceships, and other objects found in outer space. Decorate with interesting materials such as glow-in-the-dark paint, aluminum foil, and glitter. Also use your imagination to include anything you think might be found in space: Alien monsters? Giant doughnuts? It's your universe!

Next, use a pin to make a small hole in each shape you made. Tie a piece of thread or nylon line through each hole. Then, cross one dowel rod over the other at a right angle. Tie the dowels together, then tie your shapes to the dowels. Tie different shapes at different heights. Finally, tie a strong thread or piece of nylon line around the dowels to hang your mobile. You've got your head in the stars!

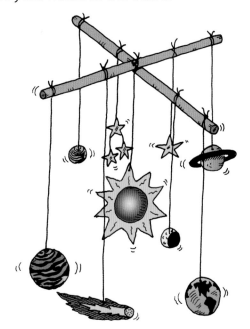

JUST HOW HOT IS IT?

Most thermometers are made with mercury, a poisonous metal. But you can make a safe thermometer using water.

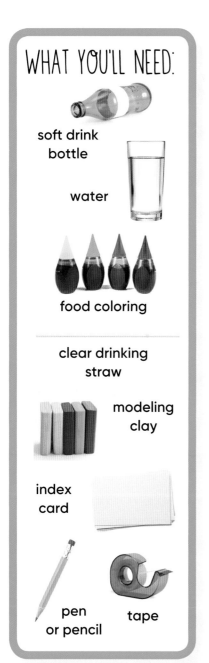

WHAT YOU'LL NEED:

soft drink bottle

water

food coloring

clear drinking straw

modeling clay

index card

pen or pencil

tape

Fill a small soft drink bottle almost full of water (about $\frac{4}{5}$ full). Color the water with food coloring. Put a clear drinking straw in the bottle so that the straw goes halfway down into the bottle. Use modeling clay to seal the top of the bottle and hold the straw in place. Tape an index card to the straw. You will use the card as a scale. Make a mark on the card to show where the water level is.

Now move your thermometer to a sunny place. Does the water rise? Mark the index card to show the new water level. (You may want to mark it with an *s* so you'll know which mark is which.) Check your thermometer at different times of the day to see how the temperature varies. You can also compare it with the weather on your local news to see if your readings match variations in "official" temperature.

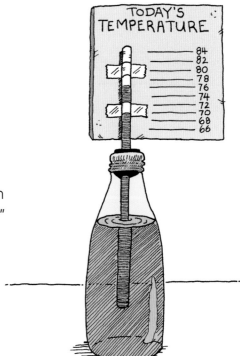

CHAPTER 4
HOLIDAY CRAFTS

HOLIDAY FANFOLDS

A folded fan can add three-dimensional interest to a flat picture in several ways.

WHAT YOU'LL NEED:

construction paper

ruler

scissors

transparent tape

markers

Cut a 3x6-inch rectangle from a piece of construction paper. Fold the short edge back $\frac{1}{2}$ inch. Turn the paper over and fold the fold back the same distance. Repeat until the whole paper is folded. Pinch one end together to make a fan shape, and tape the end to secure it.

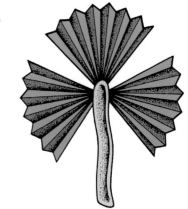

Here are just a few holiday projects you can make with fanfolds. Decorate a fan triangle with markers to make a Christmas tree. Make 2 triangles and use them for angel or bird wings. Tape a fan triangle on a turkey cutout for a tail. Make 3 triangles and tape them together for a shamrock. Instead of a bow, use 2 triangles on a present.

HALLOWEEN ORNAMENTS

Scare up a few of these recycled ornaments and start a new family tradition—Halloween trees!

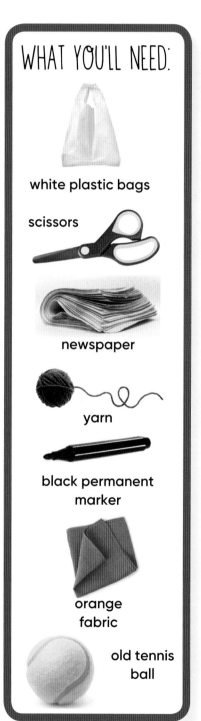

WHAT YOU'LL NEED:

white plastic bags

scissors

newspaper

yarn

black permanent marker

orange fabric

old tennis ball

Here are some ideas for rainproof ornaments made with recyclables. To make a ghost, cut a 10- to 12-inch circle from a white plastic bag. Poke a tiny hole in the center. Crumple up a piece of newspaper into a tight ball. Tie yarn around the ball, and pull the yarn through the hole in the plastic circle for the ornament hanger. Tie another piece of yarn around the plastic under the newspaper ball. Draw a ghost's face on the bag.

To make a pumpkin, cut a circle from orange fabric. Wrap it around an old tennis ball, and tie it closed with yarn. Draw a face on the fabric.

Create as many ornaments as you can dream up, and hang them on a Halloween tree.

Halloween began in Ireland as the day that marked the end of summer and the beginning of winter. It was believed that ghosts haunted the earth at this time of year, so people put jack-o'-lanterns in their windows and by their doors to scare away evil spirits. The Irish originally used turnips or potatoes for their jack-o'-lanterns, though—not pumpkins!

PAPER PLATE MONSTER

Keep this big-mouthed monster away from all your Halloween treats, or else!

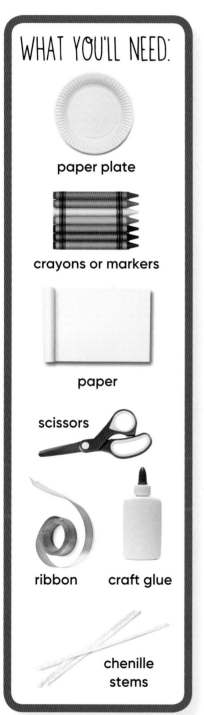

WHAT YOU'LL NEED:

paper plate

crayons or markers

paper

scissors

ribbon

craft glue

chenille stems

To make this scary decoration, fold a dinner-sized paper plate in half to form a giant mouth. Draw a few 3-inch-long arch-shaped eyes on paper and cut them out—remember, monsters can have more than two eyes! Carefully cut slits in the top half of the mouth and stick the eyes into the slits. To help the eyes stay in place, bend the bottom edges up and glue them to the inside of the mouth. Cut out antennae or horns, or use chenille stems, and attach them to the mouth in the same way you did with the eyes. Make arms, legs, or tentacles, and glue them to the underside of the mouth so they stick out. Color your monster with wild colors. You can also glue a long ribbon inside the mouth for the monster's tongue. Put your monster on the kitchen table and tell everyone to watch their treats!

WREATH OF CANDY

*Here's a wreath you'll need to hang out of reach—
or else it just might disappear!*

WHAT YOU'LL NEED:

plastic-coated wire hanger

red and green twist ties

red and green wrapped hard candy

red and green ribbon

scissors

Traditional wreaths are usually made from pine boughs or pinecones, but you might want to try something a little sweeter this year. Bend the bottom loop of a plastic-coated hanger into a circle. (You might need an adult to help you with this.) Attach a twist tie to one end of a piece of candy. Attach the candies to the hanger by twisting the ties onto the hanger. Continue doing this until you have a wreathful of candy, and then tie ribbon bows onto the wire in a pleasing pattern to make your wreath even prettier. Hang your wreath and let everyone enjoy your holiday offering!

Ask an adult for help before you begin!

SNOWMAN COOKIES

These treats are great for a cold, snowy day. Or, use them to bring a little winter to your kitchen in the summer!

Ask an adult to help you make these snowman cookies. Preheat the oven to 375°F. Remove dough from wrapper according to package directions. Cut dough into 12 equal sections. Divide each section into 3 balls: small, medium, and large. For each snowman, place the three balls in a row, ¼-inch apart, on an ungreased cookie sheet. Repeat with remaining dough. Allow space between each snowman so they have room to spread while baking.

Bake 10 to 12 minutes or until edges are very lightly browned. Cool 4 minutes on cookie sheets. Remove whole snowmen to wire racks; cool completely.

Mix powdered sugar and milk in medium bowl until smooth. This mixture is your snow! Brush it onto the cookies. Let cookies stand for 20 minutes or until set.

Using assorted candies, create faces, hats, arms, and anything else you can think of to decorate your snow people. Makes 12 cookies.

Ask an adult for help before you begin!

RAY STENCILS

Decorate a greeting card or make a holiday decoration with a simple scribble.

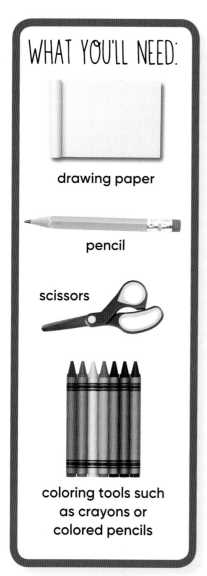
Fold a piece of drawing paper in half. Draw half of a heart shape on the fold. Cut out the heart shape along the lines, then unfold the paper. Here are a few designs you can make with the cutout heart shape and the cutout paper stencil. With the heart shape: Hold the cutout carefully on a piece of paper, and draw rays outward across the edge. With the stencil: Fill in the shape with horizontal or vertical lines, or draw small rays inward from the edge. You can make borders around a picture or overlap the hearts to make patterns. Cut out more shapes for other holidays. Use the shapes and stencils to make special greeting cards.